HEART AND SOUL

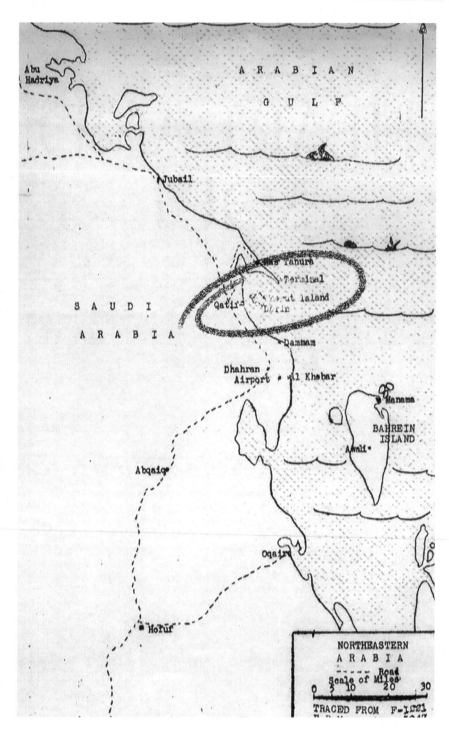

Map from the late 1940s showing the Eastern Province of Saudi Arabia, with the port of Darin on Tarut Island circled.

HEART AND SOUL

— *A MEMOIR* —

ALI MOHAMMED AL~BALUCHI

with ALISON HOOKER

Medina Publishing

ISBN: 978-191148-7555

Published in 2021
By Medina Publishing Ltd
50a High Street, Cowes, Isle of Wight, PO31 7RR, UK

medinapublishing.com

Edited by Alison Hooker
Designed by Victor Mingovits

A catalogue record for this book is available
from the British Library.

Printed and bound by Toppan Leefung Limited, China

I dedicate this book to …

My parents
My wives, Sharifa and Anisa (deceased)
My wife Amira
My children
All of my grandchildren and great-grandchildren
My sister Fatima and her children
My brothers Abdul Rahman and Jassim and their children
All my many relatives and friends from around the globe
My former supervisors, colleagues, employees and teachers

May God bless you all!

With HRH Prince Mohammed bin Salman and Frank Jungers at a special event in
Houston, Texas hosted by Saudi Aramco in 2018

CONTENTS

Welcoming friends to my home gives me great pleasure. Frank Jungers and his wife Julie have been frequent and honored guests over the years, and many Saudi retirees cherished their time with us.

FOREWORD

I HAVE KNOWN MR. ALI BALUCHI since the late 1950s, when he was selected for training in the Advanced Leadership Program offered by the Arabian American Oil Company (Aramco).

The needs of the company's employees and their families remained paramount in the years that followed, as Aramco grew. Originally, there were no Saudi Arabian cities or facilities near Aramco operations. Therefore, the company had to provide employees with living quarters, restaurants, general stores and all other necessities that would keep both Saudi and American employees happy in their jobs.

A good example during my own career was when I was put in charge of Abqaiq, one of our major work centers and communities, where I found that the community was very upset about the caliber of their feeding facilities. I obtained the services of Ali, who did an amazing job of analyzing the management problems and satisfying the needs of this sizable town. This, in turn, improved the work performance of the oil field's management, whose family needs were now satisfied. He did this by getting to know the people in the community very quickly and then doing a superb job of keeping up with and providing for their needs.

Ali also worked on some developmental assignments for key personnel within the Community Services Organization in Abqaiq to strengthen and improve their skills and performance, both within the Kingdom and in the United States. This was largely achieved through attendance at the popular Culinary Arts School of America as international students, as well as through other relevant vocational training institutions.

Throughout the duration of Ali's assignment in Abqaiq he even undertook beautification programs for the Abqaiq Community to make the town more attractive.

Ali Baluchi has continued to be a good friend of all retired employees by going to Aramco retirement gatherings, whether in the United States, Saudi Arabia or Europe. He has thus become a much-loved link between the retirees and the huge Saudi Aramco of today.

I am proud to have known Ali Baluchi as a personal friend through a period of many years.

FRANK JUNGERS

FORMER PRESIDENT, CHAIRMAN AND

CEO OF ARAMCO (1971–78)

INTRODUCTION

OVER THE YEARS, I have been invited to make speeches at many different types of gathering to very diverse audiences, from businessmen to housewives, footballers to city fathers. I would not claim to be a toastmaster, but I have observed that my listeners particularly like to be engaged with humorous stories and, most often, these are anecdotes from my own life that I feel particularly illustrate the points I am trying to make. I judge the success of these speeches by the number of times my listeners have afterwards wanted to further discuss the life experiences I shared and by the numerous requests I have received to record these stories for posterity. Hence my decision to write a memoir.

I have lived my life against a backdrop of enormous change, both in the world and in my own country, the Kingdom of Saudi Arabia. That I have been fortunate enough to navigate those changes fairly successfully is probably down to my own innate sense of curiosity and the value I see in the others I meet with on a daily basis, wherever they may hail from. From Mama Mozi, who nurtured my early spiritual development, to Frank Jungers at Aramco, who paved the way for me toward a fulfilling management career, I have many to thank for seeing my potential and setting me an example to follow in the way I approach life generally.

As you will discover, my formative foundations were laid within a strict but caring family, where there was little spare cash and I was expected to contribute to the housekeeping from an early age in whatever way I could. Despite that, my parents expected me to follow whatever opportunities were presented to me through education. My life may look like a "rags to riches" story, but it actually began with the real treasure of a somewhat traditional, hard-working family, and the importance of those family values has continued to take center place in my life. My children, grandchildren, and great-grandchildren are my greatest treasures today.

The geographical backdrop of my memoir is the Eastern Province of Saudi Arabia, known in Arabic as *Ash-Sharqiyyah*, the largest province in the Kingdom, stretching as it does along the western coastline of the Arabian Gulf. It has remained my home throughout my life. Recently, a number of scholarly histories have been published about the region and, more specifically, about the cities of Dammam and Al-Khobar, including two worthy volumes by Dr. Abdullah Al-Madani and Yousif Al-Mulla, who also contributed a number of interesting articles to the Saudi Arabian newspaper *Al-Yaum*. Another book, by Dr. Jassim M. Al-Ansari, discusses local living standards before and after the discovery of oil in the Eastern Province and looks at how the industry influenced the movements of people from other parts of the Kingdom.

My intention is not to write another history book but, as this is the geographical location in which I have invested so much of my life and energy, I hope you will indulge my reflections on the families that have contributed so much to the development of the region and the changes that have occurred here during my lifetime. Communities are built by people and we should not forget the efforts of others to create more pleasant places for us to inhabit and use, whether it be a recreational park, a football club or a hotel.

Some of my greatest joys have been found through friendship and, through the various seasons of my life, I have been blessed to make many good and lifelong friends, both locally and throughout the world. My academic studies and vocational training afforded me opportunities to travel and spend time in the United States, where I developed a strong network of meaningful relationships that I still enjoy today, now also extending through the younger generations who followed those individuals. The opportunity to travel and represent my country as a young Saudi is something of which I continue to be proud. I appreciated the chance to learn about and better understand other cultures, faiths and ways of doing things. I am convinced that this early exposure made me a more effective manager of Community Services within a diverse and multicultural environment; it has certainly enriched my life experiences and enhanced my understanding of how the world works.

You will meet many of my friends in the pages ahead, through both my own recollections and the anecdotes that they have kindly contributed. You, dear reader, may be one of them, so I hope you will see what an integral part you played along my journey. I am a relational being, so people are very important to me, even if their thoughts and opinions differ from my own. I always expect of others what I would expect of myself, and you will discover that sometimes this has even gotten me into trouble!

My life story, of course, owes much to the development of the oil industry in the Eastern Province and the journey of Saudis themselves toward taking the reins of its management. I started work for American-owned Aramco as an office boy delivering mail and messages and retired from Saudi Aramco 40 years later as a General

Manager responsible for the delivery of services including housing, sanitation, gardening, utilities and food services to the company's multiple diverse communities. It was not a progression without constant challenges, setbacks and trials, but consistent hard work, resilience and determination brought accomplishment in the end.

Much has been written about the development and achievements of Saudi Aramco as a company, but until relatively recently a great deal of the published narrative was from an American viewpoint. I present a more personal, Saudi perspective in the hope it will add some small dimension to the bigger picture and encourage a younger generation of Saudi professionals to appreciate and better understand something of the journey taken by their forefathers to pave their way. I hope a few of them may even find some useful guidance in my experiences. However, as I will reiterate later, I do feel we still owe a great deal as a nation to those early oilmen and their families who themselves made huge personal sacrifices to help develop the energy industry and the Kingdom itself.

Although it is now 30 years since I retired from Saudi Aramco, I retain strong connections with the company. It has been my privilege to advocate for the rights and conditions of other retirees, both Saudi nationals through the Saudi Aramco Retirees Committee and annuitant foreigners via the ExPats Reunion network. I became pleasantly aware quite early on that Saudi Arabia was considered home by many of our foreign staff and their families, and that it caused them considerable sadness when they could no longer return to their desert home once their contracts expired. Indeed, for their children, Saudi Arabia was the *only* home they had known before they left for tertiary studies elsewhere. Thus, the challenge of helping them to return home, if even for only a short visit, gave birth to the in-Kingdom reunions, huge logistical undertakings underpinned by massive amounts of company goodwill that consumed hundreds of dedicated hours from small groups of remarkable volunteers. I am very proud of each team's achievements and I feel honored to have had the opportunity to lead this initiative.

Now, of course, it has become easier to visit the Kingdom under the new scheme of tourist visas, and I am grateful to have had some small involvement in developing the tourism sector through my membership of the National Tourism Board. This has been just one of the numerous and ambitious reforms undertaken by HRH Crown Prince Mohammed bin Salman in his determined drive to increase economic growth and reduce dependence on oil revenues.

While more needs to be done to ensure an accurate assessment of possible economic development within various sectors of the community, it appears considerable progress is being made to improve the business atmosphere through constructive evaluations. Indeed, the Kingdom is steadily moving forward in implementing necessary reforms. Value-added tax is one example now said by the authorities to be strengthening the tax culture and new tax administration of the country. Included in the development program is an increase in financial support for smaller businesses to develop wider markets and improved financial awareness for women, following on from their welcomed gains in driving. I was delighted to discover that one of the main objectives of Saudi Vision 2030 is to encourage greater competitiveness.

Plans to reduce dependence on oil offer a healthy future environment for the Kingdom. A reduction in oil production will also leave this major resource in the ground for the benefit of future generations.

It has been a long and interesting journey, full of challenges and achievements, both for the Kingdom and for me personally.

I am grateful to Dr. Abdullah Al-Madani, Yousif Al-Mulla and Dr. Al-Ansari for their recent books and articles about the history of this region, but I hope you will find that my memoir adds another perspective. I have put my heart and soul into recording my own personal experiences and perspectives and my wish is that you join me as we retrace some of the more significant steps along the way.

ALI MOHAMMED AL-BALUCHI

~ 1 ~

HUMBLE BEGINNINGS

I WAS BORN IN SAUDI ARABIA, just a few years after the unification of the Kingdom. I grew up in the Eastern Province, along the shores of the Arabian Gulf, in what was then just a small fishing community named Al-Khobar. For most of my young life, our home was in the district of Subaikhah (meaning "saltpan"), these days known as South Al-Khobar.[1]

According to my mother, I was born in Al-Khobar on October 22, 1935. Throughout my life, she reminded me to be proud because I shared my birthday with the Prophet Mohammed (PBUH). In those days, no official birth certificates were issued, so a medical team was later tasked to address the age of citizens more accurately. As part of this process, Aramco confirmed my age and determined my new date of birth to be November 4, 1931. But more on that later.

Whenever it really was, my birth occurred in our family home. This was a *barasti* — a traditional shelter made of split palm trunks

---

1. In addition to the Baluchis, the early residents of South Al-Khobar included the following families: Al-Mutrif, As Si'di, Al-Sakran, Al-Noubi, Al-Ghanim, Al-Groon, Al-Ajaji, Al-Muraikhi, Al-Dossari, Al-Salmien, Al-Rumaihi, Al-Yagout, Al-Jowair, Al-Ali, Al-Hoti, Al-Khamis, Al-Abdullatif, Al-Fyza' and Al-Maglooth.

with plastered walls and a thatched palm roof. The plaster was a lime mixture derived from crushed seashells. It was a common building technique throughout the Gulf region at that time, often used by the Bedouin in summer months when they came for the cooler coastal weather.

Because most of the houses were made of palm fronds, we knew our neighbors very well. Even in the 1950s, most of the residents of Al-Khobar were on fairly close terms. Most families had small doors cut between their houses and those of their neighbors to enable easy access; this way the women could visit freely without having to use the main entrances of their homes. Over the years, as conservative religious norms became a more dominant influence and both Saudi men and women aspired to become more sophisticated and "modern" in their behavior and dress, it became necessary to create and maintain more privacy between families within the community. Sadly, it is no longer common practice to retain a passage between neighbors.

I remember there being many mirrors on the walls of our *barasti* house; my father loved decorative mirrors. I used to enjoy posing in front of these until one day my grandmother came into the room and caught me at it! She wasn't impressed, but I continued to be quite fascinated by my reflection.

Another lasting memory I have of my grandmother was that she kept a lot of chickens in our yard. Inevitably, they created a lot of waste and dirt there, making it both difficult and unpleasant to walk around the house perimeter. Eventually, I had had enough and decided to persuade my grandmother to get rid of the unsanitary offenders. The following day, however, my wily grandmother cooked two delicious eggs for me to eat to convince me of their value. I then kept my complaints to myself for a while. When my grandmother later became frail, my mother cooked one or two of the chickens every Friday until they were all eaten. My grandmother passed away in June 1960, at which time I was attending a summer program at Bucknell University in the United States. I was very sad when Aramco, my employer, did not approve my request for a short leave so I could attend her funeral.

One of my very earliest memories involves my Uncle Ahmed taking me to the port on Darin Island (now better known as Tarut Island), off the coast of Al-Qatif. I was only about three years old, but I can still recall the boats coming and going into the harbor at sunset as we watched from our vantage point on top of a huge water tank. At that time, there were few local water wells, so the government transported water via a big traditional dhow from a seawater well near Jubail. I was always curious about how the fresh water came from under the sea. When our family moved from Darin to Al-Khobar, I remember we sailed on a dhow — it took a couple of hours but was a comfortable and safe voyage.

At the beginning of World War II, our family was living on Darin Island. The disruption to shipping caused by the conflict resulted in food shortages, so the government distributed a variety of food items such as rice, oil, brown sugar, flour and tea to the inhabitants. We were quite surprised by the generosity of the government at the time as it had no regular income of the kind that future oil revenues would endow.

I was very young and the global war was of no concern to me, but I do recall that my father spent many hours listening to the radio news. One day, in October 1940, while he and his friends were sitting in the living room listening to the radio together, I heard them talking about an Italian air strike on the new oil company community in Dhahran; some bombs had been dropped and they were worried about the impact. They were apparently concerned that the Italian air force had intended to strike the oil and gas refinery in Bahrain. Later, I heard a friend of my father tell him that the Italian leader apologized to King Abdul Aziz Al-Saud for the air strike, claiming it was a mistake.

The sound of the bombs dropping scared the residents of Al-Khobar and the nearby villages and created shock across all the communities. It impacted the expatriate workers too, and my father reported that many of Aramco's American families were subsequently shipped out by boat to Bahrain and then on to safety in the United States.

The radio was always very important in our home, and we would listen to the news and music from other Arab countries, especially Egypt. My father always invited our friends and neighbors to join us. In the 1950s, these "old-timers" particularly loved to listen to the speeches of Gamal Abdel Nasser (President of Egypt between 1954 and 1970) and the music of Umm Kulthum, a very popular singer in the Arab world. Those men spent many long hours gathered around that radio, drinking tea and coffee while they listened.

Our family later moved to a home constructed of stones and mud. By the early 1940s, the local living conditions were still tough and hard to cope with, but it was all that was available — we had very little choice. The quality of water, housing and sanitation was far below any of the acceptable standards we take for granted today. Electricity for domestic use only came to South Al-Khobar in 1954 and was certainly not reliable. Consequently, we were exposed to many potential environmental health risks, but people just accepted the situation as there was no alternative.

Because we had no electricity, we would sleep on the roof during the summer to try to catch a breeze. It was sometimes so humid that I can remember as a child waking up soaking wet and thinking that someone had thrown a bucket of water over me. Our first air-conditioning unit was only installed (somewhat euphorically) by my family in 1962 after I purchased and brought it from the United States while studying there. The landline telephone followed in 1963, installed with the help of a gentleman named Mohammed Sultan.

For entertainment as children, the neighborhood kids and I played a lot of soccer. We played in the streets and on open lots, using stones for goal posts. I was not particularly competitive at the time, but soccer went on to become a lifelong passion of mine.

Throughout the 1940s, Al-Khobar's King Khalid Street used to turn into a small lake after heavy rains. All the local kids would find half-barrels and fashion them into makeshift boats, rowing them across the "lake" for fun. We did this for many years until the street became an important thoroughfare in the town. For those of you familiar with Al-Khobar, the seashore at that time came very close to where the fish and meat market is today. An artesian water well was drilled by Aramco in the same area, from which my father used to haul water to our house.

The year 1943 witnessed heavy storms throughout the Gulf region. The locals named it *sannat attaba'h,* meaning the "Year of Drowning," due to the loss of so many lives, fishing boats and commercial vessels. Al-Khobar itself experienced 40 consecutive days of severe winds and storms. Sand covered the entire neighborhood and our whole community (the area now called Bayouniah) had to be evacuated and relocated to another quarter near the seashore. The Director of the Municipality encouraged everyone from the affected area to take as much land as we could, so my family claimed a large section. It was here that our family first had a permanent stone house. Later, when some friends of my father came by and asked for a piece of our land, my father kindly gave it to them. However, they still had to pay the municipality certain fees.

A few years passed and my father decided he needed to retrieve one of those land grants in order to build a house for my older brother. The owner was asking 5,000 riyals for it but, in view of his original generosity, my father asked if he could buy it back at a discounted price. The owner categorically refused, arguing instead that "whatever the market dictates, you have to pay!" So, my father paid the market price.

I recall one occasion when, while still a youngster, I happened to meet Abdul Wahab Salamah, the Director of the Al-Khobar Municipality. He encouraged me to ask my father to invest in real estate in Al-Khobar since it was affordable and reasonably priced. When I suggested this to my father, he responded: "If I had extra money, I would rather buy a sack of rice for my family!"

MEETING MY FIRST AMERICAN!

In the mid-1930s, an American named Scott Harrison conducted a survey of Al-Khobar as the potential site for a residential camp for expatriate oil company personnel. He copied the street layout of Manhattan, New York, numbering the street grids in a similar way.

Harrison was the first American I ever saw. I had gone to work with my father in the Customs Office at the port one day when I noticed an unusually tall man wearing a hat and talking to Mohammed Al-Zahid, who was a surveyor from the Municipality. I asked father what was happening, and he explained that the tall man was an American named Mr. Harrison who had come to survey our little town on behalf of his employer, an oil company from America. For whatever reason, it seems Aramco eventually considered the Jebel Dhahran, a group of rocky hills further inland, as a better site for the construction of its company headquarters and residential family camp.

Despite this decision, Aramco still had a major role in the ongoing development of Al-Khobar. It became one of the first cities in the Kingdom with water and sewer systems (a Dutch company was brought in to start the project in 1963). Frank Patterson from the Aramco Home Ownership Program also had a great impact on the development of several notable communities in the Eastern Province and his role was well recognized and much appreciated by both local authorities and residents. The Home Ownership Program was quite significant as it was specially designed for Aramco's Saudi employees, being one of the early incentives to attract and retain young Saudis to its workforce, especially those with an education.

The modern communities of Dammam and Al-Khobar are considered to have been founded by Sheikh Ahmed bin Abdullah bin Hassan, leader of the Al-Dossari tribe from Bahrain, in about 1923. Sheikh Ahmed reportedly had an excellent relationship with the founder of modern Saudi Arabia, King Abdul Aziz Al-Saud. Sheikh Ahmed died in Dammam on May 20, 1949. Sheikh Mohammed bin Rashid Al-Amour Al-Dossari and Essa bin Ahmed bin Sa'ad Al-Damookh Al-Dossari are also commonly considered as founding fathers of Al-Khobar.

For a while, Al-Khobar was known as the "Pearl of the Arabian Gulf," and the town became increasingly attractive to people from Bahrain and further afield. Well-known family names included Al-Dossari, Al-Gosaibi, Al-Faraj, Al-Nassar, Al-Khuzaim, Al-Hassan, Al-Zain Alabideen, Al-Mani, Al-Zamil, Al-Madani, Al-Matloob,

Al-Nagadi, Al-Hulaibah and Al-Majid.[2] These families brought a tremendous abundance of experience, knowledge and money to develop and modernize the town. Many other residents came from the various regions of the Kingdom, bringing different cultures and expertise. In my humble opinion, they did very well in developing Al-Khobar into a modern city in such a relatively short period of time.

Other important families of note include those of Abdullah Al-Hamad Al-Zamil, Abdul Aziz and Saleh Bahussain, Abdul Aziz Al-Turki, Mohammed Al-Faraj, Hamad Al-Gosaibi, Ali Abdullah Al-Tamimi, Mohammed Al-Mazrou', Mohammed Al-|Tamimi and Abdul Latif Al-Fuzan. They are still known as the biggest families in business, real estate, factory building, establishing technologies and generally providing employment through economic institutions that serve the whole Kingdom. These families have also contributed significantly to building our community through sponsorship of philanthropy, educational and social programs and the building of mosques. Their achievements have further extended to the facilitating of faculties and halls in some universities. Educational and science centers like the Sultan bin Abdul Aziz Science and Technology Center (Scitech) in Al-Khobar and Prince Mohammed bin Fahd University in the Eastern Province also owe their existence to the generosity of these fine businessmen.

King Abdul Aziz also helped with the early development of the Eastern Province by providing a substantial number of educated citizens from the Western Province to run and operate various

---

2. Well-known families from Bahrain and other nearby Gulf countries included Al-Dossari, Al-Hassan, Zain Al-Abideen, Al-Shukri, Al-Khan and Al-Madani. Families who came from Al-Zubair included Al-Mani, Al-Gosaibi, Al-Faraj, Al-Nassar, Al-Khuzaiam, and Faisal Al-Majid. From the Hejaz came the Al-Matloob, Al-Nagadi, Ismail Qaburi, Ali Al-Abyadh and Sowayigh families. The Al-Khobar families of Al-Madhi, Al-Tamimi and Al-Zamil (to name but a few) originated from the Najd region.

government agencies, such as Customs, Finance, Post, Cable and Wireless, and Municipalities. I remember some of these: Yousif Al-Tawel at Customs, Ismail Qabori at Post, Saleh Al-Suwaigh at Cable and Wireless Communications, Abdul Wahab Salamah at the Municipality and Saleh Islam at Finance and Economy. Hassan Al-Khuja ran the Al-Khobar Customs and Major General Hassan Ghanadily headed up the Police. Others included Ali Al-Ghamdi, Principal of the Al-Amiriyah School of Al-Khobar.

It is interesting to note how, over many decades, much of Al-Khobar has expanded as a result of land reclamation from the sea. This is because no one owns the sea. To buy land for development, even if it seems just like open desert, is expensive. There is always someone who claims prior ownership. Now, of course, there is also growing sensitivity to the environmental issues surrounding reclaiming land from the Gulf.

~ 2 ~

FORMATIVE FAMILY FOUNDATIONS

MY FATHER, Mohammed Ali Al-Baluchi, was born on Darin Island, close to Al-Qatif in the Eastern Province of Saudi Arabia.

Our house was in the Subaikhah area of South Al-Khobar and my father would relax there by smoking hubbly-bubbly. On one occasion, while he was smoking, I asked him why my grandfather had decided to settle down in Darin Island. He said his father was like so many Saudis of the time who were forced to travel away from their roots in order to make a living. My grandfather had travelled from the Buraimi Oasis when Buraimi was still under Saudi rule. Father cited several other well-known examples of people who had become economic migrants, including Abdullah Al-Zamil, who travelled from Unaizah to Bahrain, and Al-Bassam, who went to India. Many others travelled abroad to places such as Zubair (Iraq) and Kuwait for the same purpose. Consequently, both my father and his only sister had been born in Darin Island.

Father married three times. After he had been married and divorced twice, he decided to travel back to Buraimi to search among his relatives for a bride. He succeeded by finding my mother, Maryam. She was much younger than him and she eventually gave birth to two boys and one girl. He stayed with my mother as she was the last woman he married.

My lasting impression of my father is of a consistently hard worker. Unfortunately, he was also a heavy smoker for most of his life. Growing up, he had no access to formal education. When he was 17, because he was very fit and strong, he accompanied his close friend Saif Mu'dhadi to take work as a pearl diver with a Dubai merchant named Abdul Aziz Al-Ghurair. Their contract required them to stay on the merchant-owned dhow out in the Gulf waters for three to six months at a time, diving and searching for pearls. I can still remember some of the occasions when the local pearl divers would return from their long voyages and the whole community would turn out and celebrate at the seashore to welcome them home, their wives all wearing their best dresses and makeup. At that time, their makeup consisted of henna for the palms of their hands, ground rose for the cheeks and basil leaves braided through their hair. Their lipstick came from a plant root known as *dairem*.

The dhow captain gave my father two French riyals (coins known as *riyal faransi*) before he left for the diving work so he could buy supplies for the family to sustain them while he was gone. On the day my father passed away, he put his head in my lap and asked me to please repay this loan. Later, I went to Dubai and found the pearl merchant, Sheikh Abdul Aziz Al-Ghurair. I told him why I was there and presented him with the money. He assured me there was no debt to repay because all of his success was due to the hard work of my father and his many other divers. He assured me it was he who should repay the debt to me. He even asked if I was married because, if not, he could find me a bride. He must have considered me very trustworthy!

After being a pearl diver, my father worked with the Saudi Coast Guard (under Salim Al-Rushaid) and then as a Customs House guard, first in Darin, followed by Uqair, Qatif, Dammam, Darin again and finally Al-Khobar. My most vivid memory of his time with the Coast Guard is of when he took me with him on a donkey between Al-Khobar and Dammam. Unfortunately, I fell off and was told in no uncertain terms that he would never take me with him again!

Father was later transferred to the position of Senior Customs Inspector at the Al-Khobar Customs House. It was in this role that he came to witness at first hand the influx of vast quantities of oil drilling equipment with the early American geologists and Aramco employees. It quickly became clear to him that this was to be the way of the future. Apparently, while previously working at the Uqair Customs House, an American oilman had offered my father a job, but he turned down the opportunity, believing he would have more job security working for the Saudi government.

Once the Aramco School had been established in Al-Khobar, however, my father was keen that I should attend it to learn English. He did not speak English himself but wanted to ensure his son did.

In 1942, my father travelled to Makkah by camel. It took him 60 days. In the early 1940s, there was only one vehicle in town that I can remember — a 4x4 pick-up owned by Hamad Al-Dossari, which was used to deliver fruit and vegetables on a daily basis from Qatif to Al-Khobar to sell in the market. I believe it may have originally been donated to him by Aramco, although his son Khalid said the family bought it in Bahrain. One day, my father asked the driver, Faraj Al-Dossari, to let me ride with him to Qatif so I could drink some buttermilk and taste a piece of *gubaith* (a sweet made of flour, sugar, date syrup and peanuts). It was a memorable trip — my first ride in a vehicle! I thought, "This has to be better than donkeys and camels! This is an upgrade!"

A LOCAL CURE

Around that time, my father became ill and went to seek help from a doctor. There was one in Al-Khobar at that time, an Indian gentleman. He gave my father a variety of treatments, but they all failed, which concerned me. I pondered how I might help.

During the summer months, all the young boys and girls would attend what was known as a "sit-in school," where we sat on the floor while studying and learning to recite the Holy Quran. This was done under the leadership of a well-versed lady teacher who was traditionally called *mutawa'h*. When a student completed the full course and was able to recite the whole Quran, the group would visit all the houses in the community and sing religious songs, celebrating the occasion. Most of our entertainment then revolved around these types of religious activity. Later, as I grew up, I continued studying the Quran during the summer months with Sheikh Mohammed bin Sahal, who was also Imam of the Grand Mosque of Al-Khobar, the only mosque at that time.

It was in fact the mother and aunt of Abdullah Jumah (later Saudi Aramco President and CEO) who gave me a copy of the Quran and taught me at their house with other local kids. The aunt was known as Mama Mozi. In those days, young boys and girls were mixed together in these groups, making it my first co-educational experience.

While I was attending one of these summer Quran recitals, I mentioned my father's sickness to Mama Mozi. I told her how, on the previous day after I had finished the class and returned home, I had observed him in severe pain. He was tired of taking medicines, and the doctor could not diagnose the problem. I asked for her advice.

Mama Mozi suggested I take my father to her mother, Um Mibar, who was known for successfully using a special healing treatment of burning. This involved heating a bar of metal on the fire and then placing it on whichever part of the body she identified as important for promoting healing. When I discussed the treatment with him, my father admitted that he was by then "willing to go through any kind of treatment to get well". (With the benefit of hindsight, I believe that my father was probably actually suffering from sciatica.)

The next day, I took my father to visit Um Mibar and we were received by her children, Othman and Al-Himily. After we had been served coffee and dates, my father underwent the procedure. I could hear his cry of pain whenever she placed the stick of hot iron on the designated places on his body. Eventually, he completed the treatment and we left Um Mibar's house. My father suffered considerably while the burned parts healed but then, after a week or so, he forgot all about the pain and recovered. He passed away on January 9, 1964, and in all the intervening time, I never heard him complain of that sickness again.

For many years, my father continued to smoke hubbly-bubbly, but it gradually damaged his health. Once, when his friends were visiting him in our newly built living room, I heard one of them ask him anxiously how long he would continue smoking, and at that point he agreed to stop. However, after a few days, he became quite ill, coughing a lot. I took him to Aramco's Emergency Clinic, but he was denied treatment as he was ineligible. We then tried the Al-Sharq Hospital (now the Mohammed Dossary Hospital) in Al-Khobar, where the doctor told him he should not have given up smoking all at once but rather cut down gradually. Unfortunately, father wound up suffering from asthma for the rest of his life. He was typical of most old-timers, who don't really care about the consequences of their choices and rarely make changes.

AT THE CUSTOMS HOUSE

Father was a strict disciplinarian. Each day on my way home from school, I would stop by his office at the Customs House to greet him. One day he said, "Ali, I want you to take a message to my friends Mohammed Al-Tamimi and Mohammed Al-Mazrou' in Al-Khobar. Say hello to them and tell them I am doing fine." In order to make sure I went fast enough, he spat on the ground and told me I had to be back before the spit was dry or he would spank me. I ran so fast to deliver the message — in fact, I had to carry my shoes and run barefoot for greater speed — that, when I got back, my father could tell I had tried my best and did not spank me. However, he did chide me for not wearing my shoes!

There was always something interesting going on at the Al-Khobar Customs House and many opportunities to learn something new. For example, once when I was visiting on my way home from school, my father introduced me to a businessman named Abdul Rahman Al-Rashid. He was carrying a large spool of thread and an enormous needle, so naturally I asked him what he was intending to use them for. He was flattered by my interest and patiently explained that, whenever a tear or hole was discovered in the sacks of imported rice or other foodstuffs at the port, his task was to re-seal or mend them so that the rice or other food products would not be lost.

I recall another time there was a visit to the Customs House by some businessmen accompanied by the Governor, or Emir, of Al-Khobar, Sheikh Mohammed bin Madhi. I shook their hands while father was conducting an inspection. Another regular visitor was a man called Mousselini (we all knew him as that, but he may have had another name), who delivered ice to the Customs House staff while meeting Aramco employees at Al-Khobar pier on their way into the Kingdom from Bahrain. I believe the ice may have been some kind of bribe or sweetener.

In those years, the government collected taxes from cigarettes, and a stamp would be put on each packet to show that the tax had been collected. This was done at the Customs House, so I often helped father and his co-workers with the task. I was able to collect a nice little income but gave it to my father to help support my family.

AN ENCOUNTER WITH THE GOVERNOR

One particularly memorable incident from father's time at the Al-Khobar Customs House involved his dealings with a businessman leaving the Al-Khobar pier with a donkey-cart laden with toys. At that time taxes were raised from imports and *zakat* (the mandatory Islamic charitable contribution) and were the only source of government revenue. On this occasion, however, because the toys were for children, my father decided not to identify the items as objects for which he should charge a tax.

Word of this clemency reached Prince Saud bin Jalawi, Governor of the Eastern Province, who immediately summoned my father to his palace in Dammam. The governor criticized him for his actions and placed him under house arrest in the Aramco Saudi General Camp for a few days, under the supervision of a police officer.

By the next day, my family was anxious that father hadn't returned home from his visit to the palace. I hurried to Dammam myself and insisted on a personal audience with the governor.

Unfortunately, the manager of the governor's office was Ali Al-Ghamdi, who had previously been the principal of Al-Amiriyah, the school in Al-Khobar that I attended as a child. I knew he could be a strict man to deal with. He was not sympathetic toward my seeing the Governor about my father's case as he felt I was far too young for such an important meeting with His Royal Highness. Regardless, I continued to insist on a personal audience with the governor, so loudly that his office manager warned me I risked bringing the prince out of his office to see what was going on. I asserted that "I don't care! I want my father. I must ask Prince Saud to release my father."

My persistence paid off and I was finally allowed in to see the governor, who was in fact very welcoming and kind. He greeted me, shook my hand and asked his servant to offer me some tea. He listened to my story but then gave me a long lecture. He said, "Your father is known as an honest employee with a long service history: He has worked in the ports at Uqair, Dammam, Qatif and Darin. But the government depends on customs revenue to run the country."

"Where is my father? I can't go home without my father."

"Your father will be home in two days," he replied.

However, I continued to entreat him to let me see my father.

The prince finally asked his driver to take me in a red pick-up to the Saudi camp (Aramco General Camp) where my father was in custody. When we were reunited, it was an emotional moment for both of us. He was staying with a police officer but was fit and healthy — a relief for my mother, who wanted to know what had happened as soon as I got home. I explained to her that he would be released in two days, which was indeed when he returned home, as His Highness had promised.

During his early years in office, Prince Saud bin Jalawi ruled the Eastern Province with an iron fist. During the toughest part of his governorship, it was common for thieves to be punished by having their hands cut off for their crimes. Often, the authorities would hang the severed hands or feet of the perpetrators on the fence of Aramco's Main Gate into Dhahran as a deterrent to others. It was very scary to see this in public after finishing our work each day, and it had the intended effect! Despite this, however, Prince Saud generally governed the Eastern Province effectively. I believe his mandate was to govern in a way that would create a safe environment in which both locals and foreigners could satisfactorily work and live alongside one another. In my opinion, he performed his task well and generally brought peace of mind to the population.

MY FATHER'S PASSING

In the later years of my father's life, as his health deteriorated, I volunteered to help him with family affairs. He agreed, but I soon discovered that it was not very practical or wise to take on this responsibility while he was still alive. When I admitted to him that the task was proving somewhat unworkable, he told me he was very happy to take back his obligations.

I was privileged to be with my father when he passed away on the afternoon of January 9, 1964. He was 60 years old. I am sure his life was shortened by his constant hard work with little access to health facilities, rest or vacations.

Before he died, he asked me to serve him orange juice from a can so as not to bother mother for a clean glass. He made several other requests of me, including asking me to look in his wallet for 50 riyals to give to a local food store to clear an outstanding debt. He intimated he should be buried before dusk, and that his shroud should be the gown he had saved from his Hajj pilgrimage to Makkah. He further requested I treat his friends nicely after his death and, as already mentioned, that I travel to Dubai to settle his old pearling account of two French riyals with Sheikh Abdul Aziz Al-Ghurair.

Father also reminded me to look up his friends from Qatif, specifically mentioning the families of Shammasi, Jishi, Al-Faraj, Al-Sinan, Al-Khinazi and Abu Saud. He respected their friendship and their hard work over the years to provide fruit and vegetables to the people of the Eastern Province.

Father then died peacefully, his head in my lap.

When he asked me to bury him before sunset, I had expected it to be a major challenge as I was unsure where I would find an undertaker to prepare his body for the burial services. Surprisingly, three people arrived for that purpose. It was a big relief, as we were now able to bury him before sunset after all. Father had owned a Persian rug that he loved very much, spending a couple of hours every Friday cleaning and brushing it. I decided to cover his grave with this.

The family held a dinner to honor my father's life and memory. We were blessed by the presence of his friends, acquaintances and neighbors — about 500 in all — joining us to mark the occasion.

While still living, father had divided the family home between all of his children and my mother. He gave my sister a bigger piece of land, which led to objections from others in the family. However, once I had returned from my out-of-Kingdom training in the United States, I was able to persuade the family to agree to my father's decision.

MY BROTHER ABDUL RAHMAN

No account of my family would be complete without mentioning my older "brother," Abdul Rahman, as he played a major role in our family as I was growing up. In fact, he was my uncle, my father having taken him into our family when he married my mother. Our father's income was not adequate to fully support us all so, as he was in effect the eldest, he carried a heavy load in helping to maintain the family's living standards.

Abdul Rahman behaved as if he were our godfather. He was a very strong and self-disciplined person, working initially as an artesian well driller and later as a carpenter. He knew just how to handle my sister, brother and me, and from time to time was even known to intervene to get us back on the right track. He invested a great deal of valuable time in helping me to become more independent and, by virtue of his constructive guidance, I was able to conduct myself in a much more commendable fashion as I grew up. He showed me how to navigate the growing local community as a well-behaved youth. All the credit goes to Abdul Rahman, my father consistently respecting and reinforcing his role as my mentor.

I recall one amusing story someone shared with me regarding a time when Abdul Rahman was hired by the Ministry of Agriculture in Jeddah. Apparently, on one occasion while he was travelling by air with a fellow worker, the plane hit a storm, so frightening his colleague that the poor man tried to sit in the aisle for the duration, thinking it must be the safest place to sit until they reached their destination!

MOTHER

My mother's name was Maryam. She came from the Al-Buraimi Oasis in north-west Oman, close to the present-day border with Al-Ain. There, her parents farmed dates, mangoes and lemons. As a child, I took a few trips with my family to visit my grandparents, a journey that involved boats to Dubai and then travelling by camel or truck to the oasis itself. Sovereignty and jurisdiction over this area was disputed for many years, but it eventually passed out of Saudi influence in 1974. My grandfather, however, refused to recognize the changes and continued to cling to his Saudi nationality throughout his life — as evidenced by his Saudi National booklet (identification card) being found under his pillow on the day of his death!

My mother was considerably younger than my father and was a very attractive woman. Even I found her looks very striking — I had to lower my eyes when I talked with her. As I was her eldest son, she was known to all as "Um Ali" (Ali's mother). She was charming and well-liked by the community and used to gather and host many local ladies at our house several times a week. If someone failed to appear, she would call and reprimand them. Being very religious, she gained most of her pleasure from discussing and reciting the Holy Quran. While breast-feeding her own children, she was also wet-nurse to many other boys and girls from the various communities in which she lived. In Islamic teaching, if a woman breast-feeds children not of her own body, those non-siblings become relatives — consequently, I am now known as "Uncle" by many of those people.

When guests visited the house, even if they were looking for my father and he was away, mother would warmly welcome and entertain them. Her cooking was legendary, and as we had no maids back then, she would spend hours in the kitchen preparing meals. I will never forget one of my favorite dishes, known as *saloona*, similar to a stew and made from a delicious variety of vegetables, chicken or lamb.

When I was about six years old, my father took me to visit Sheikh Ibrahim Al-Khan, a popular tailor in Al-Khobar, to have him make me the national dress in preparation for the holidays. My father asked him to have it ready for the Eid holiday, even though this was still seven months away! When I eventually picked up my outfit, my mother was very pleased with it, but then surprised me by asking me to store it flat under my mattress. When I asked her why, she replied that it would then be nicely pressed ready to wear during the holidays.

At one point, mother needed open-heart surgery and was referred to the King Faisal Specialist Hospital in Riyadh. Her doctor from the Dhahran Hospital warned us that, because of her age, they might not be able to perform the operation, but she told Dr. Hassan that she was not too old and was ready to undergo the procedure. When I discussed the matter further with a visiting doctor from the United States, he assured us that he had survived open-heart surgery at a much more advanced age than my mother.

In the end, mother came through her operation successfully and lived another 20 years, reaching the age of 86 before passing away on December 19, 1999. Although I spent time with her every day on my return from work, I now wish I had spent more quality time with her prior to my retirement. After I retired, I continued to be so busy with community and business interests that she complained I never had enough time for her.

I was raised to have very strong family ties — we were encouraged to stay close to our family so everyone could help one another. I believe I also gained an early understanding of the importance of community from the example set by my mother.

AN ELEMENTARY EDUCATION

AS I HAVE ALREADY MENTIONED, when I was young it was common practice that, when a child reached five or six years old, the family would enroll them in a traditional "sit-in school" to learn to recite the Holy Quran. Most fathers worked or strove to build a profession to sustain their families. Many were engaged in the popular but demanding work of pearl diving, so, while they were away for long periods, mothers were left to manage family affairs.

Because of this, it was quite normal for parents to grant a teacher permission to discipline and train their child. There was even a popular saying used by many parents at that time to exhort the teacher: "You have the flesh while the bone is ours." This meant that the teacher was permitted to use whatever means necessary, including beating the child, if he deemed it would accelerate the learning process and improve performance. A child could also be physically disciplined for failing to do his or her homework. It may seem strange to us now but, in those days, families generally approved of harsh punishments for their children.

I recall that, when a child missed class, the teacher would send two or three other children out to find them. Their search would always include the seashore and the places where we liked to go hunting for birds. When they found the truant, they would carry him back to school in disgrace. Of course, the teacher had the green light to punish that child — "you have the flesh!" Parents' prime motivation was for their child to learn and come home educated. In some cases, parents would complain to the school about their child's misbehavior at home, requesting that the teachers administer the appropriate punishments.

There was, however, still a correct way of doing things. One teacher recounted to me the consequences he experienced when a particular family appeared to have failed to register their child at school on time. Apparently, the father had actually informed the school's principal of the reason but somehow the information did not filter down to the child's teacher. As a result, the teacher scolded the boy and the boy reported this to his father. The father loaded up a pick-up truck with members of his tribe and came to the school demanding an immediate and full apology from the principal and staff!

Although a child might achieve the skill of reciting the entire Quran, it did not mean they actually understood the meaning — only that they could memorize well. The achievement allowed him to graduate and a party would be planned for him to celebrate. He was dressed in a nice *thowb*, gown and headpiece with sandals and a golden sword. The early part of the day was for the graduate, his family and family friends to enjoy. Some would then carry a variety of dishes of food, an incense burner and some rose water in its fancy dispenser to the school. Once at school, everyone would gather and applaud the graduate as he sat in the place of honor with his father and his teacher beside him. To begin the graduation party, one of the students would recite from the Quran, the rest of the students answering with a resounding "Amen." After that, everyone would leave the school to visit the graduate's neighborhood, where they would receive gifts. It was an important event in the community.

I underwent this whole process during my early years. Other than the Quranic schools, there were very few schooling options then on offer for the majority of children. I was fortunate enough that my parents followed my Quranic education by enrolling me in the first primary school in Al-Khobar (Al-Amiriyah), which I attended from first through fourth grade. As time went by, more schools became available, and Aramco helped with the establishment of some of these. Most often the new schools were in rented buildings.

Before school, I would wake up to pray and then my mother would make eggs and bread with tea and cream for breakfast. There was no electricity in our house, so the breakfast was cooked over a wood fire. My local school was a mile away, and I walked there along dirt streets.

A general education consisted of Arabic reading, writing and spelling, religious courses and study of the Quran. I had about 15 classmates and every one of my teachers was tough: They took no nonsense from their young students. My classmates then included Khalid Al-Dossari, Ahmed Al-Dossari and his brother Abdul Rahman, Sa'ad Ahmed, Ibrahim Abolkhail, Saif Husseini, Suliman bin Essa, Khamis Dhahi, Nahar Nassar, Khalifah Ali and Khalifah Eid, to name but a few.

At that time, the principal of the school was a certain Mr. Maghrabi, but he was later replaced by Ali Al-Ghamdi (the gentleman who went on to become the Office Director for Prince Saud bin Jalawi, Governor of the Eastern Province). Al-Ghamdi was a severe disciplinarian in his position as school principal and a firm believer in collective punishment. If a few students were absent on any day, even if they were living in different villages, he would assume they had conspired not show up and would punish them accordingly. I was among the happiest of students when Al-Ghamdi was reassigned and replaced by Abdul Hamid Al-Mubarak. Unfortunately, however, Al-Mubarak was killed a year later in a motor accident while performing the Hajj. He was a highly respected person in the area and well-liked by both his students and the local community. He had married a woman from the Al-Dossari family in Al-Khobar.

My primary schoolroom recollections include that of Nahar Al-Nassar pretending to be an airplane pilot in the classroom one day. Nahar later went on to attend Aramco's Jebel School with me. With the encouragement of his father, Abdul Razaq, he fulfilled his dream, pursuing flight training as a career through the Armed Forces. He eventually became a special pilot for both King Faisal and King Khalid — just one of my classmates who achieved so much because of the opportunities Aramco afforded us through the Jebel School and beyond.

Doing homework was not without its own hazards in those days. One eventful night while I was studying at home, my father suddenly shouted, "There's a fire in the house — something is burning!" I was shocked to discover it was actually my hair that was on fire! For domestic lighting we would use a Fanta bottle filled with kerosene with a thread or wick protruding from it, which we then lit. The wick was held in place by liquid dates, as we had no glue. Distracted by my enthusiasm for my studies, I had not kept myself far enough away from the light and accidentally set fire to my hair!

THE NEXT STEP

When I was in the third grade, Aramco came to the school and hired all the students from the year above me. My father was very interested by this, as he had previously heard about Aramco training programs and he hoped that one day I would be able to join one. During the early 1940s, Aramco built a small school in a *barasti*-style building in Al-Khobar to enable Saudis to attend English classes in the evenings. With my father's encouragement, I attended the Saudi school during the day and went voluntarily at night to the Aramco School to study English. There were no entry tests for the night school as it was open for anyone to attend (males only, of course) — we were just encouraged to go and take the opportunity to learn.

The night school was constructed close to the government's wireless and cable station, which used the power supplied by the school's generator to run its equipment and electric lights. For the first time in my life I was able to experience electric lighting!

In 1946, after I had been attending this evening school for a year, Aramco selected 10 students to continue their studies at its Jebel School in Dhahran.

I was one of those fortunate students.

~ 4 ~

TRANSITIONING
THROUGH TRAINING

I CAN STILL RECALL that special night in early June 1947 when Mr. Hamza Amody, the principal at the Aramco night school, announced the selection of a number of students as potential candidates for employment at Aramco. I was thrilled to be one of those selected. More detailed information followed, and it included the news that we would also be enrolled at the company's Arab Trade Preparatory School on a part-time basis, with the company undertaking to provide the necessary transportation to and from Dhahran. Mr. Amody asked us to share the offer with our parents and then let him know our answer the following evening.

My parents enthusiastically welcomed the opportunity afforded by this extra schooling since there was, at that time, just the one primary school in Al-Khobar, this only delivering education from first through fourth grade. The government offered students an opportunity to further their studies in Hofuf, but my parents were reluctant to let me go there as I was too young to stay there on my own.

The Arab Trade Preparatory School was popularly known in 1947 as the "Jebel School." *Jebel* is the Arabic word for a hill or small mountain, and the school was so named because of its location in the shadow of the mounds left by the erosion of the Dammam Dome geological structure. Situated in the area used for the early Dhahran exploration camp, and close to the present-day Al-Munirah Commissary facility, it was nothing very grand by today's standards. Our trade school was housed in a coral-rock-and-plaster building that had previously been used as a bunkhouse. There were no asphalt roads to it at that time.

I believe I was in my early teens when I started as a student at the Jebel School. (As I have already indicated, there was some question over my exact date of birth.) The administrative assistant at the school suggested to me that I might need to increase my age, otherwise the oil company would not hire me as a regular employee or student. When I went home, I told my father about this age issue. The following day, he took me to Sheikh Hamad Al-Gosaibi, a prominent businessman in Al-Khobar. Sheikh Hamad asked his son, Suliman, to go with me to the local National Identity Office to tell the director there that he remembered when I was born.

When the director duly asked Suliman my age, he replied as instructed. The director accepted this and issued a new ID certificate with my birthdate as 1931. The Aramco Recruiting Office was most pleased to receive this new certificate because it was desperate to attract young Saudis to work for the company, especially those with some education, or at least those who could already read and write Arabic. That is how my date of birth became November 4, 1931.

Thus, I found myself attending the Jebel School on a part-time basis from September 1947. I was just a teenager, so I was pleased to discover that all my fellow students were also still only boys and not yet grown men. Although we were students at the company school, we were not Aramco employees — the company just provided us with free schooling for half days, with no salary or benefits. The company did, however, transport us each morning and afternoon between Al-Khobar and the school in a 4x4 truck. This truck was covered with a canvas tarpaulin to protect us from the dust and harsh sun and had hard wooden seats that were very uncomfortable. Still, the discomfort paled against the excitement of the new experience and the promise of a career with an oil company — at least we hoped a career would be at the end of it all.

My first supervisor was Waddyi Sabbagh. He was from Iraq and held the position of administrative assistant at the Jebel School. He was well-equipped to take care of the students because he spoke Arabic, allowing him to help with interpreting between us and the Aramco supervisors and American teachers. We studied religion, English, accounting and shorthand. I was in the same shorthand class as Ali Al-Naimi, who progressed most successfully through his career to become the President and CEO of Saudi Aramco, and then the Kingdom's oil minister for more than 20 years. Aramco arranged with the governor of the Eastern Province to assign a number of teachers of Arabic — some of those I remember were Hamad Al-Jassir, Mohammed Towfiq, Mohammed Shaibani, Saleh Maghrabi and Al-Malhouq.

Before attending the Jebel School, I spoke only the little English I had learned at night school, just a few words that were enough to help me safely get by. Most of my English was gained through the American teachers at Aramco's Advanced Training Center and later by going to college in the United States.

There was a small crowd of us from Al-Khobar who went to the Jebel School. I recall this group included Saif Al-Husseini (a lifelong and close friend), Abdul Rahman Al-Dossari, Ahmed Al-Dossari, Khalid Al-Dossari, Sulaiman Al-Gosaibi, Sa'ad Ahmed and Khalifah 'Eid. As previously mentioned, I also met Ali Al-Naimi and many other young Saudis like Khalid Al-Turki, Suliman Gimlas, Ahmed Al-Zamil, Ali Al-Zamil, Abdullah Busbait and Fahd Qaslan. As we progressed to work for Aramco and rose up through the ranks, we continued to share many experiences of travel, study and working life. Some of these young boys went on to start their own businesses, becoming successful contractors to Aramco in their own right.

Before we could be offered employment with Aramco, however, we had to complete at least one year at the Jebel School, starting each day at 7.00 a.m. and finishing at noon. These half-days of training, preparing us for a specific job, would continue for at least another year once we were employed. The Aramco philosophy was very clear: They were not providing education as a social service. Rather, they put you through a training program in order to meet specific job requirements. The company maintained this approach for a number of years but was eventually forced to become more flexible in response to the pressure of facilitating more Saudis into key company positions.

Anyone who has ever spent 10 minutes with Ali Baluchi can testify to his dynamic personality, his charisma, and his tremendous level of energy. Those were traits I first noticed many, many years ago, when we both attended the Jebel School.

H.E. ALI AL-NAIMI, ADVISOR TO THE ROYAL COURT
(FORMER MINISTER OF PETROLEUM
AND MINERALS, 1995–2016)

Jebel School students who had fathers or uncles already working for Aramco received a payment of 90 riyals per month. I was not so fortunate, so, until I could gain such employment with the company, I had to find some other work to help my father support our family. Hence, I worked as a salesman at the Green Flag store when it first opened in Al-Khobar. I also worked as a typist with the Eastern Company, and some nights I helped my father and his colleagues at the Al-Khobar Customs House by posting the import stamps on cigarettes.

A TOUGH LESSON

A lasting and formative memory of my time at the Jebel School involves me and one of my classmates, Ibrahim Abolkhail. On this particular day, we were distracted during class and just generally goofing off together. Our teacher, a Bahraini named Mr. Yousef Al-Hassan, was upset by our behavior and told us that we would be suspended and docked three days' pay.

I was upset and didn't want to tell my parents that I was in trouble. Instead, I went to personnel to discuss it, and they agreed the punishment was too harsh for the misdemeanor. However, the teacher insisted. It was then decided to leave the matter for the judgment of Sheikh Saleh, who came from the Dammam Governor's Office to the school to teach us the Quran and religious studies. When Sheikh Saleh heard the story, he decided that we actually deserved *seven* days' suspension without pay! The school chose to settle for the three days and naturally we concurred.

When I told my father, he was pragmatic and said it was a very good lesson. He felt that I was learning the necessity of respecting authority and that I should always behave myself around others.

I do indeed consider this one of the best lessons of my life and, from there on out, I never got into trouble again, always working hard and paying respectful attention to both my teachers and others in authority.

Many years later, that same Bahraini teacher called on me. He was near retirement, working for Aramco as a Stock Controlman in Ras Tanura. He was anxious about an opportunity to be promoted and to be given a house in Dhahran, close to the main gate so he could quickly get to Bahrain. Much to his surprise, I told him, "Mr. Yousef, I'll never forget you because you gave me three days' suspension without pay and those three days probably made me a much better man. It could be that those three days also made me a better employee, a better citizen, a better father and everything else."

I called Ahmed Al-Hazza, who was the head of Material Supply and a good friend of mine. I asked him for his help with Mr. Yousef's circumstances: I wanted him moved from Ras Tanura to Dhahran with a promotion that would enable him to relocate into housing near the hospital in the main camp, thus making it easier for him to get to Bahrain. Happily, we were able to expedite this well before he retired.

THE COMPANY MEDICAL

Prior to joining the company's service, we were all required to undergo a medical examination, which included a thorough physical. When I shared the matter with my father, he gave me very specific instructions about refusing if the doctor asked to examine my private parts. If he insisted on the examination, I was to drop the employment application and return home, because this invasion of my privacy was contrary to our culture and my father's interpretation of our religion.

The next day, I shared my father's strict instructions with the principal of the Jebel School, Mr. Vince Quinn. He discussed the matter further with Don Richards, the superintendent of schools. Mr. Richards then assigned Vince James to accompany me, driving me in a company pick-up. He was tasked with accompanying me during the medical examination and other related employment processing to ensure my father's wishes were respected. I did, however, allow the doctor to do a full examination, although I couldn't tell you exactly what he did. Overall, I felt he had respected my father's requirements.

At the end of the day, my father was waiting to hear how things had progressed and especially about my physical examination. I took pains to reassure him that the doctor was very pleasant and that I had been accompanied throughout by an American whose job was to ensure his wishes were respected. He just smiled.

Some 30 years later, I met Vince James in the United States while attending one of the American Annuitants' Reunions. I asked him why he had helped me undertake my employment processing. He said that Mr. Richards, his boss, had threatened that "if Ali changes his mind and declines the company's employment offer for any reason," Vince wouldn't get his next raise and it would reflect on his work performance assessment. He went on to reiterate that, in those days, finding a Saudi who already had some level of education was viewed by Aramco as a "gift from God."

Just before my dear father passed away, one of the things he talked about was my Aramco physical examination for employment in 1949. He turned toward me and said, "I know you did not tell me the truth at that time, but I forgive you." Then he said, "Who are you for the company to change its rules?" We both smiled and, shortly afterwards, he left us.

VISIT BY KING ABDUL AZIZ AL-SAUD

On one occasion, as I was making my way to school, I observed a great number of people on the roads putting up street decorations in the various areas we passed through. Later we were told that King Abdul Aziz Al-Saud was visiting the Eastern Province for the second time. During his visit, he attended events in Dhahran, at the Ras Tanura Oil Terminal and in the Najma community. The Saudi company employees also hosted some special parties to mark the occasion with entertainment for the local children. On his way home, the king also visited Al-Hasa and celebrated with the residents there.

I recall the school students standing along the sides of the main street to welcome the royal entourage. During his visit, each student received a gift of 30 riyals in appreciation. This was a lot of money in those days.

My father eventually got the opportunity to see the king at a special event he hosted for a select group of officials from various government departments. It was on the last night of the royal visit and was held close to the site of the present US Consulate General in Dhahran. The people of the Eastern Province were very excited to meet the man who had united the Kingdom.

When I talked afterwards to Americans who had met King Abdul Aziz Al-Saud, they were impressed with him as a person, finding him humble and welcoming to both Saudi citizens and the company executives and their families, especially the children. I recall a Mrs. Kriesmer telling many of us about how American families from across Aramco were invited to meet the king and were requested to wear long dresses and hats. Their party was held at the old Dhahran Ball Field, along the King's Road. My father told me that Sheikh Salman bin Hamad Al-Khalifah of Bahrain came across to visit the king too and attended a dinner in a hotel in Dammam hosted by the Governor of the Eastern Province, Saud bin Jalawi. Aramco threw a big party at the Dhahran Dining Room. The community got to hear about it all in detail later from Ali Suhaim, who was a Saudi supervisor at the Dining Hall and a resident of Al-Khobar.

As part of his visit, the King also attended the 1946 Soccer Finals for the MacPherson Trophy, a match between local teams, the "Dhahran Union" and the "Somalis," with the latter winning 2–1. I had wanted to attend that game but could not manage it due to a lack of transportation. Later, Sheikh Hamad Al-Ubaidly proudly told a group of us how the king had presented him with a trophy in recognition of his "Union" team achieving the accolade as the best team overall throughout the 1946 season.

MY FRIEND, SAIF HUSSEINI

My close friendship with Saif Husseini was one of many formed when we first enrolled in the Jebel School in 1947. Saif received 90 riyals per month because his father was already an employee of the company, but I had no relatives working for Aramco, so I did not get paid. It was not until I officially became an employee, on February 15, 1949, that I received the same amount.

Over the years, he and I participated in a host of shared activities. When he was sent to Lebanon and Aleppo in Syria to study for his degree (which he finally obtained at the American University in Beirut), I visited him and his dear family multiple times, getting to know his children well. We travelled together for numerous vacations in the Middle East as well as to the United States and Europe.

Saif particularly enjoyed visiting Cairo and did so several times each year. One time, when I was particularly missing him, I asked him to return to Saudi Arabia with the promise that I would take him out for breakfast every Thursday for 20 weeks. (At that time, the Saudi weekend was on a Thursday and Friday. In 2013 a royal proclamation changed it to Friday and Saturday to enable alignment with other countries in the Gulf region.) When he finally returned to Saudi Arabia, I kept my promise, never changing the number. I so enjoyed his company.

Throughout our friendship, we shared our sporting interests: While I played soccer, he handled much of the club's administration work. In 1967, when I was elected the President of Al-Qadisiyah Sporting Club in Al-Khobar, he became my Vice President, going on to succeed me as President when my four-year term concluded.

I was very sad when Saif passed away. He had gone to Cairo for a dental appointment, but the next evening he became very ill. The emergency doctor at a local clinic suggested treatment, but Saif decided he would rather return to Saudi. He called his children to help him return home, but by midnight he had been declared dead at his Cairo apartment. The Saudi Embassy stepped in to help the family, preparing all the necessary documents and arranging for the body to be shipped to Dammam. When his body arrived, the burial customs were observed over the following three days.

So ended our deep and strong friendship. May God bless his soul.

MARY NORTON SHARES THE IMPORTANCE OF LOYAL FRIENDS:

One of Ali Baluchi's strongest traits is loyalty to his friends. His closest friend was Saif Al-Husseini, who told me how he and Ali frequently met for breakfast in Al-Khobar. Saif was also a dear friend of ours, [and] remained so long after our retirement. Since he passed away, I have been touched to see Ali's occasional memorial posts about Saif on Facebook. Ali also penned a lovely tribute to another dear mutual friend, Nasser Al-Ajmi.

~ 5 ~

I'M HIRED!

FEBRUARY 15, 1949 was the date I started working for Aramco, on the grand salary of 90 riyals per month. Once the formalities were completed, I was assigned to the office of the Superintendent of Schools, Mr. Don Richards, as an office boy. His secretary, Mrs. Marsha Naylor, was my immediate supervisor. Initially, I worked in the office for four hours a day, spending the remaining four hours with the study program.

In this position, I was expected to deliver mail and messages between the offices for the superintendents of schools and training and to work as a typist. I found myself laboring alongside a Pakistani gentleman who was quite reluctant to teach me typing because he was worried that I would take his job. During the lunch hour, when this man left the office, I would retrieve wastepaper from the trash can and use it to practice my typing. Eventually, when my skills had sufficiently improved, I did replace him, and he subsequently left the country. Many years later, the man contacted me and asked if I would sponsor him to return to Saudi Arabia for work. I agreed, but only on the condition that he teach his job to two Saudis while he was here. He agreed to the arrangement, and then worked in the Kingdom until he retired.

My boss, Don Richards, bought me a bicycle to help me deliver mail more efficiently between the different Aramco office locations. Each Thursday, he encouraged me to take the bicycle home with me to Al-Khobar to have fun with it and enjoy it over the weekend. I took it once and was somewhat bemused to find myself riding a bicycle from Dhahran all the way to Al-Khobar. It was something I had never thought of doing before. The outward ride proved relatively easy because the inclination is downhill but returning to the Aramco camp on that bicycle was a lot more of a challenge! I decided that trying it the one time was definitely enough. I remember Don Richards as a very nice guy. I later heard that, when he retired and moved from the Kingdom, he went back to the United States and became the head of the Chamber of Commerce in Bakersfield, California.

I gave all the money I earned to my parents. However, my father used my first paycheck to buy me a watch — a West End-style watch from the Al-Khobar shop "Shukri." Later, my mother saved up my money so she could go to Makkah for the first time.

Once I became an employee, things started to change. For starters, I had to travel between Al-Khobar and the Aramco facilities with the other local workers in a big open truck. This was only used for the transportation of employees early in the morning and late in the afternoon; the rest of the day, it was used for hauling pipes and cement. On two days in the early 1950s I was late and missed the Aramco truck — then I had to walk for eight kilometers!

Besides me, my friend Saif Al-Husseini and the other trainees who lived in our area used this free company transportation. As well as the workers from the labor pool and those toiling in the Aramco trade shops and drilling, there were accountants from the small accounting office and IBM. Because the truck was open to the elements, I would often get to work covered in sand and dust. On one particular occasion, my immediate supervisor, Mrs. Naylor, stopped me as I arrived and asked, "Where have *you* come from?" I told her I had just come from Al-Khobar. She replied that I looked more like I had just come out of the desert! "And," she observed, "it looks like you've encountered a lot of difficulties to get here along the road from home." Of course, my hair was full of dust and cement. I assured her it was only that we had been transported in that same big, dirty truck that Aramco usually used to haul pipes and cement. She immediately sent me to the restroom to get cleaned up.

I was privileged that Mrs. Naylor regularly allowed me to use the washrooms designated for management. I only experienced one incident during my career that felt at all racist. Not long after I started working, I happened to quench my thirst at an indoor drinking fountain and was promptly told that the drinking facilities were segregated for Arabs and non-Arabs and, as an Arab, I was required to drink instead from the one outside!

When I started working for Aramco, my father was quite insistent that I continue to wear Saudi garb and not change to Western-style clothing. One day, Mrs. Naylor returned from her vacation in the United States and Spain with some nice trousers, which she gave to me as a gift. However, my father was determined I should not wear them and told me to keep them at home. Then, in 1951, my father moved from customs work to the National Guard. I came home from work one day and found him smiling, which was unusual as he was a tough man who did not easily smile. I asked him, "Why are you smiling?" and father replied, "You win. Today we were told at work that we all have to wear Western dress, so now you can wear the Western dress you received from your boss too."

I was so excited that I wore my new trousers to work the very next day, even though I didn't have a shirt to go with them — only a thobe that I tucked into the pants. Mrs. Naylor took me to Don Richards to share the news, but it was a while before I was able to spend my 90-riyal monthly salary on a couple of shirts.

Western-style dress only really began to be worn by school students in the 1960s. In a very short time, tailors of many different nationalities started opening shops in Al-Khobar. Each tailor publicly displayed their certificates and diplomas to attract the young Saudis. As time went by, more shops opened with clothes imported from overseas; I recall one in particular called "Al-Arabi Al-Saudi," which was owned by the Al-Saie family from Bahrain. Other stores were owned by Lebanese and Syrians, but their prices tended to be very high and they were clearly catering to wealthier families. I tended to favor the Indian and Pakistani stores, with their more reasonable and attractive prices.

THE ROOTS OF SAUDIZATION

Many people think that "Saudization" is a relatively recent initiative, but it actually became part of the Aramco company ethos in the years immediately after World War II. Many programs were launched to train Saudi nationals as skilled tradesmen and workers and to fast-track them into professional and managerial positions through company-sponsored university education.

In 1950, Aramco phased out the Jebel School and elevated it to become the Advanced Industrial Training Center (AIT). The American teachers there included Helen Stanwood, Elli Keenan Beckley, Ralph Sherman, Earl Beck, Bill Grebin, Mr. Ownby, Mr. B. Schroeder, Bill Koeneke, Mohammed Farouqi and Vince Quinn. This hard-working team engaged us young Saudis in a program of math, English, spelling and penmanship (writing), shorthand, typing and accounting. Their task was to prepare us to increase our value as employees. Wadyi Sabbagh continued as the administrative assistant at AIT, and Abdul Rahman Al-Dowaihi was our counselor.

Our Saudi teachers numbered amongst them the famous Saudi historian Sheikh Hamad Al-Jassir, Mohammed Towfiq, Essa Ashoor, Yousef Al-Hassan and Saleh Maghrabi. Another teacher I remember well was Mohammed Shaibani, who later became Deputy Minister for Information. Religious studies included conducting and performing daily prayers during school hours, and these were led by Sheikh Al-Jassir.

Many of AIT's students were identified and mentored for further educational opportunities abroad a few years later. The program was intensive and well-planned, specifically designed to prepare the young Saudi participants for a wide range of future challenges and opportunities.

Running parallel to AIT, another center was established, called the Industrial Training Center, where selected Saudis were trained in more technical and vocational skills such as plumbing, carpentry and electricals. A number of its graduates went on to become notable foremen at Aramco, including Hussein Farhan, Abdul Monim, Khalil Younis and Saleh Qabqab.

I recall being invited to attend a special gala dinner in late December 1950. Held in the Dhahran Recreation Portable, the purpose of the event was to mark the achievements of Aramco's Education and Training Section. Hosted by Don Richards and his wife, it was a pleasant gathering, although I wasn't very well-versed socially at the time! There were a lot of important company personnel present, including Mr. Fred Davis, who was the company president at the time — I believe they used to call him the Chief Company Resident. Don Richards was my "big boss," although in reality my effective boss was his secretary, Mrs. Naylor. Wadyi Sabbagh, the Administrative Assistant, and Essa Ashoor, one of my teachers, were amongst those who gave speeches during the evening's program.

Aramco has long considered training to be essential for developing the skills and knowledge of its employees to meet the various and changing needs of the workplace. I remember my father telling me when I was a small boy how he had once encountered a group of about two dozen Saudis being sent through Al-Khobar port to Bahrain for training purposes; I believe that was probably one of the first-ever Saudi groups to be sent abroad on a development plan.

In its early years, the company's objective was to train people for specific jobs. It was only in the 1960s that the objective began to shift toward more generic development of Saudis recognized as having leadership potential. Certain Saudis were selected to go to study in the United States with the understanding that, upon successful completion of their programs, they would commit to remaining with the company for a number of years. Failure to do so would require repaying the company all expenses associated with the plan.

The earliest well-site training was mostly given on a one-to-one basis, with a foreman sharing his skills and knowledge with his individual workers. Industrial training programs were then developed to speed up the knowledge-transfer process, especially in drilling. I recall two gentlemen by the names of Mr. Osborne and Mr. Cooney being kept busy training particularly large and strong Saudis in drilling work. Out of necessity, other skills-related training programs quickly followed, including welding, electricals, carpentry and accounting.

Aramco always expected its Saudi workforce to work hard on improving both their workplace-related skills and their knowledge of English, which was the company language and used operationally on a daily basis. Any opportunity for Saudis to progress would take into account the level of their communication skills. As a result, many attended night school. I can still recall one American employee commending the 25 percent of the Ras Tanura Saudi workforce who, in the 1950s, were attending school in their own time at company training facilities.

I had a conversation about training with Harry Snyder (who had been appointed in 1949 to oversee training of Saudi recruits) just before his retirement from Aramco and move to become a prominent consultant at the King Fahd University of Petroleum and Minerals. Snyder was pleased with the progress he made in fulfilling the company's objective of developing the capabilities of Saudi employees to operate effectively throughout the whole oil-production process. The goal was eventually to achieve complete operational management by a national workforce. Snyder claimed he had achieved "most of that in five years," but qualified the accomplishment by saying "there is a still plenty of room for more training."

Aramco's vocational training program extended to a school of nursing started by John Miller, with an initial enrolment of 10 Saudi nationals. Miller's training program was of three years' duration and graduates received a Diploma of Nursing. Some were then sent to Lebanon for two years to obtain nursing degrees. The participants included Sa'ad Abdul Karim, Ibrahim Abdul Aziz, Tahir Abdullah, Abdul Aziz Al-Mubarak and Hassan Al-Nasser, the father of Amin Nasser, the current Saudi Aramco President and CEO.

At some point, I attended the driving school established by Aramco to teach safe driving skills to its Saudi workforce. The school was located near the present Al-Rashid Mall in Al-Khobar. I believe Bob Dunlop may have been the last supervisor of the school.

It is important also to give Aramco credit for training up many of the Saudis who were employed by Saudi contractors. In 1953, the company opened a training school for some of these workers, initially concentrating on welding skills. Aramco's objective was to develop a pool of local talent and, in so doing, over the years the company was able to effectively direct more and more of its activities through local Saudi contractors.

COMMUNITY LIFE

My first encounter with Aramco's Community Services occurred during the 1950s. Through its Recreational Services I enjoyed a variety of what were, for me, formative cultural experiences. I believe these experiences rooted in me the deep personal interest and desire to share in the lives of those in our expatriate communities, as evidenced by my continued commitment to this for the rest of my life. I also started to gain an understanding of the importance of a healthy community life for all.

While still a young man without family commitments, I became very much involved in the Dhahran community. I spent numerous long evenings with many other volunteers in decorating Building 510 (the "Quarter Riyal Meal" Dining Hall for employees in Grade codes 3–10) for various occasions, even some religious events. I became very adept at seasonal decorating and my interest in recreation and food services grew, especially during the Christmas and New Year holidays. The credit goes to three ladies in particular: Mrs. Hauk, Mrs. Dell'Oro and Mrs. Naylor. They were very enthusiastic, kind and supportive.

I have fond memories of frequent invitations given after these social and decorating events to visit various homes within the Dhahran residential community for late dinner and refreshments. During this time, I also became involved in organizing various sporting efforts amongst the young residents. These included soccer, basketball and badminton.

As time passed, I also helped Aramco extend athletics support to soccer teams throughout the wider communities of the Eastern Province. This took the form of donating uniforms and providing transportation whenever there was a game or competition between teams in different areas. Some of the Americans involved were Mike Ameen, Carl Jackson, Bob Long and a Mr. Sutherland, who were very instrumental in sustaining this kind of backing and support.

It is most satisfying that Saudi Aramco's assistance for local sports has continued to expand and flourish through the decades.

~ 6 ~

A MATTER OF FAMILY

MY CLASSMATE, ALI AL-NAIMI, found a good wife who became a huge support to him. This remarkable lady, Dhabyah, came from a prominent Bahraini family. My first wife also came from Bahrain. It was common to look for a wife in Bahrain because of a shortage of women to marry in the Eastern Province. This was partly due to increasing competition over them from fellows coming from other regions to work for Aramco. I recall there were also a number of prominent personnel from our local government offices who went to Bahrain to marry, including the head of Al-Khobar Customs and the head of the Post Office, Ismail Qabori.

In those days, when looking for a potential match, the woman's family was a more important consideration than the woman herself: You also had to take into account her tribal heritage and the family's reputation. Parents could be very fussy about who their son might choose: They wanted to be sure that their son was marrying someone from a respectable family and a decent tribe, and who had a good reputation. Consequently, it could sometimes take a while and a lot of searching to find a suitable wife.

Shortly after I joined Aramco and started work, my father became consumed with the urgency of finding me a suitable wife. The concept of getting married early was common at the time and pursued enthusiastically by all the local parents. The added probability that those *boys* who had just joined Aramco might be sent overseas for education and training provided another incentive to get married sooner to "protect" them against possible foreign temptations!

My father raised the issue with me and, of course, I gave him my full consent to pursue the matter. My parents then embarked on a massive search to find me a suitable wife without any actual involvement on my part. In other words, my mother would fall in love and I would get married! Over an extended period of time, my mother and sister zealously conducted numerous investigative visits to different families in Al-Khobar, Dammam, Jubail and Bahrain, their task protracted by the challenges of transportation around the region.

The young lady who was to be my intended bride was named Sharifa. She lived with her mother in Bahrain, while her father conveniently worked and lived in Dammam. When my father and I set out to visit him to pay Sharifa's dowry (2,000 silver riyals), I clearly recall complaining that the money bag was much too heavy for me to carry. Father merely retorted that, if I wanted to get married, I would have to carry it, otherwise I should forget about the wedding. I said "fine" and got on with it. We finally made it to Sheikh Mohammed A'bubshait's house and concluded the marriage deal in the presence of my father and the bride's father.

Although each of my wives has come from outside of the Kingdom, I subsequently came to desire that my own daughters should marry Saudi citizens in order to sustain our own community.

I also took the initiative and challenged the dowry system, making dowries obsolete within my own immediate family — I made the dowry requirement only one riyal for each of my daughters!

My wedding took place in Bahrain. My mother and sister accompanied me by sea to the island, where we were met by Sharifa's uncle. He welcomed us and blessed the marriage. The dowry was delivered to him and the ladies began the wedding arrangements. As per tradition, I had still not had the opportunity to see or talk with my future life partner and had to wait patiently until the wedding night.

The following morning, my mother and my sister Fatima came to ask me if I was happy with their choice of bride. I replied, "It's too late now. Thank you and I will live with the situation. That's my luck." However, I did also thank God and pray that my wife and I would have a loving and prosperous life together. They insisted that in time we would grow to love each other, just like everyone else did. I performed the Bahraini tradition of a trip to a local park to have a bath and, over the following days, friends and family gathered to present us with gifts and money.

During the early years of our marriage, Sharifa and I lived with my parents in their house, staying there until my father's death. "Um Saleh," as my wife came to be known, quickly became the "unknown soldier" in our family — she endured a great deal, taking on the biggest role in caring for our children while selflessly giving me the opportunity to study and progress at work. She did eventually object, however, when I suggested taking on a PhD in Medicine! I owe my career progression to her.

When our first child, Fouad, was born, he received a great welcome into the family. Sadly, however, he was taken from us in his first year by a severe bout of diarrhea. When he became sick, we took him to the Dhahran Hospital, but they told us to take him home as there was nothing they could do. Fouad died shortly thereafter. This was a very sad time for everyone in the family, but especially for Sharifa and my mother.

It was two years later that my daughter, Faiza, was born. Schooling for girls was not generally available in Al-Khobar until the 1960s, so in 1959 we sent her to Bahrain, where education was more readily available for girls. She lived on the island with her grandmother, Halima. At school, the girls were encouraged to experiment with developing their culinary skills, but there was not much health and safety awareness in those days, and I can still recall an accident my daughter Layla had with a pot of very hot water — she had to be rushed to hospital for treatment. After two years, Faiza was able to return to Al-Khobar to attend a newly opened school for girls. She went on to work as a teacher before giving it up to look after her six children.

Since I was constantly busy with building a career, Sharifa took the responsibility of handling our family matters. I was, however, able to be present at the birth of all my children except Hussein, who was born while I was abroad. Upon my return, I saw a little boy, asked who he was and had to be told he was my son. That was an unforgettable moment.

Our life was simple, organized and strongly connected with our local family, friends and neighbors. The Al-Muraikhi, Shaheen, Al-Mutrif, Yaqout, Khudher and other families became like an extended family to us. Thanks to Sharifa and my mother, all of our relationships with family and friends were characterized by great loyalty and compassion. Despite me being away so often, Sharifa also ensured that all our visitors coming from Oman or the Emirates were greeted with warmth and provided with a comfortable stay.

My wife continued to urge our children to study hard and to excel in their education. As a result of her relentless efforts and perseverance, the girls became fully qualified as teachers and the boys all became leaders in their respective fields, thanks be to God. At the same time, she continuously supported my pursuit of advancement at work and further educational opportunities while providing me with a comfortable and happy environment at home.

When the kids grew up and reached an easier age for us to leave them with others, Sharifa and I were able to travel together as a couple and visit with our many friends. We enjoyed staying at our friends' homes in the United States and the Netherlands.

Our family always came first. I recall an example when Sharifa had to undergo heart surgery in the United Kingdom. The doctors requested that she take an extended recuperation period in London, staying close to the hospital for effective monitoring. Sharifa, however, insisted on returning home just one week after the operation to oversee the marriage arrangements of our youngest son, Hamdan. She attended the wedding party while in a wheelchair but was very happy, and she later told me that the night had made her feel the happiest mother ever.

Throughout our life together, we never found the need to agree on a set monthly allowance to meet the daily household requirements. I would provide her with whatever she requested as our financial situation allowed. She was a consistently loving person, maintaining a compassionate relationship with her family, and constantly looking out for their welfare. On several occasions, and without my knowledge, she even sold some of her own jewelry to provide help for some of her more needy family members. I never objected, though — I knew just how caring a person she was.

In addition to our own kids, there were another three children whose welfare and upbringing Sharifa, with my mother's help, looked after. Zubaida was brought to us after her mother, my cousin, passed away. Two years older than my daughter Faiza, Zubaida was so affectionate with my kids, growing up like an older sister to all of them. She became particularly attached to Hamdan and, when she got married, she requested that Hamdan go to live with her in Qatar. Sharifa accepted and blessed this request without hesitation and, for five years, Hamdan lived with Zubaida. It was only when she gave birth to her first son that Hamdan returned home. Zubaida still lives in Qatar along with her six children and her wonderful husband, who we consider an older brother to the whole family.

The other two children who were raised under the care and guardianship of my mother and Sharifa are my nephews Anwar (son of my brother Qassim) and Khalid (son of my sister Fatima). They joined us after their respective parents separated. Sharifa looked after them as if they were her own, with a motherly passion and care.

Sharifa was ever mindful of and grateful for the many things our children enjoyed during their childhood that others never had. Thanks to my trips to the United States, where I had first experienced many of these things myself, we were amongst the first and few in our community who owned a television, fridge, electric washing machine and telephone. I made sure that my family was able to take advantage of these technological developments.

I have so many precious memories, but whatever I write or say will always fall short of describing the true character of Sharifa, Um Saleh, my beloved first wife. We were blessed to have four daughters — Faiza, Layla, Hind and Aisha — and five sons: Saleh, Hussein, Mohammed, Isam and Hamdan. We have been further blessed with many grandchildren. I strongly believe that all the good fortune bestowed on us by God the Almighty is in great part due to Sharifa's patience, loyalty, faithfulness and perseverance, and her relentless and unhesitating efforts to provide maximum support to the family.

In her last few years, Sharifa was plagued with ill-health, requiring ongoing medical assistance and intervention through several surgeries. A few days before her death, I asked my children to call all of their aunts and uncles — Sharifa's sisters and brothers — so that everyone was together at 10:56 p.m. on January 1, 1997 when I received a call from the Aramco hospital informing me of her death.

Sharifa will never be forgotten and will always be missed, not only by me and our children, but by our all relatives, neighbors and friends. My beloved Sharifa, my dearest Um Saleh; may God the Almighty compensate her with His full mercy and forgiveness, and grant her the best place in heaven.

As I have said, Sharifa was a natural mother and our home was always filled with children, sometimes as many as 17 at a time! One was my nephew Khalid, who has kindly shared the following memories with me of "Umi Sharifa". *Umi* is the traditional way of referring to one's mother.

> *While the house was full of kids and lovely noise during the day, when Uncle Ali returned from work, we all became so well behaved and obedient. Umi Sharifa would never complain about our noise or the trouble we may have caused her during the day. She had the big responsibility of taking care of a household full of kids and always hosting relatives and friends, but she would never hold back, even if she was ill or tired.*

*At nighttime, all the kids, grandparents and Uncle Ali
would surround Umi Sharifa while she passed out bread
to us with a piece of cheddar cheese and a cup of tea with
milk … . I was always fascinated by the swift way Umi
Sharifa used the manual can opener to open the cheese
can and cut it into pieces, a skill I always hoped to achieve
but never perfected. There was always an extra piece that
she slipped into my hand in a hidden move, a gesture that
gave me both great joy and a full stomach. I miss those
evening gatherings very much but the sweet memories of
them are engraved on my heart.*

*Umi Sharifa's harshest form of punishment or
reproach was to avoid looking at me. There would be
no smiles, no special gifts of cheese or jam, and no
assignments to the bakery or grocery store. It was so
effective that even my own mother would then be angry
with me. I would stick beside her with eyes to the ground,
waiting for her [to] smile and point her finger warning
[me] not to repeat the mishap again. I didn't keep all of
my promises, but she never stopped forgiving me. She was
standing behind me when I received the news of the birth
of my first child, and the joy and happiness that was on
her face as she congratulated me was unforgettable —
I will always cherish that moment.*

KHALID AL-BALUCHI

*It is quite hard to share my memories when they concern
my mother, but there is one event that is vivid in my
mind. It happened when my son, Mishal, completed the*

sixth grade. When she heard about it, with a big and
happy smile, she gave him 1,500 riyals. It was her own full
allowance that she had just received from my father at the
time. We, my wife and I, really appreciated the gesture.
It showed us the extent to which she was willing to give
just to make us happy.

SALEH AL-BALUCHI, ELDEST SON OF ALI

Although this chapter has mostly been about my wife and family,
I feel this is an appropriate place to follow Khalid and Saleh's memories with a piece from my son Hussein about the kind of father he
has found me to be.

MY FATHER'S HAPPINESS IS MY CROWN: THOUGHTS FROM HUSSEIN ALI AL-BALUCHI

It is not an easy thing to recall all the great memories
I have from the 1960s onwards, but here are a few threads
of memory about my father that express the appreciation
and the love I hold for him. The great care he showed me
during my upbringing is indescribable, as he was in equal
part father, friend and mentor.

The earliest memory I have is from the time of my
grandfather's death when, even though he carried all the
responsibility of heading up the funeral process, my father
was able to spare the time to spread fun amongst us kids,
distributing bananas and bread. On my first day at school,
understanding how nervous I had been about going, he was
in the first row waiting to meet me at the end of the day.

Father worked hard and moved between different areas that kept him away from home for extended periods of time, but that never prevented him from ensuring we maintained our studies and persevered to reach the highest educational success we could achieve.

He inspired us to take up leadership responsibilities and to be socially active within our society, fostering our involvement with his guidance and the right push when needed. I followed his example and joined the Al-Qadisiyah Club, serving as a club council member for three seasons. Father encouraged us to provide help whenever we saw a need and to give a hand to whoever was in need of assistance. He has always been a problem solver and my siblings and I are now learning from him how to find effective solutions to challenges we encounter.

One of his most admirable acts was the rule he set in the family with regard to my sisters' marriages, when he insisted that their dowry should not be more than one silver Saudi riyal. No one else in our family, or the region, had done that before. He set an example in helping to change and reduce the heavy burden of the marriage cost that young people carry.

With his continuous care and interest in the family's affairs, he creates a great relationship between all of the family members, both close and distant relatives. Always present for the joyful events, my father will be the first to share their sorrows. We strive to imitate him and maintain the same kinds of relationships. He is a great role model to his many grandchildren, always staying in touch with them, keen to hear from them and engage in colorful moments with them.

Father has a habit of assigning each of us with special tasks from time to time, carefully following up until the task is completed or, if not, we had better have a good reason for not completing it. As an experienced investor, he has encouraged us to invest in real estate in order to maintain a good living standard and future prospects for the family. His golden advice is to be a good listener, let others express their points of view before reaching conclusions, and always respect and listen to our elders.

My father is respected and appreciated by His Highness the Emir of the Eastern Province and by other dignitaries, prominent businessmen, and all the social and community leaders. He earned this admiration and respect through his hard work and efforts to be a magnet of kindness and practicality as well as a strong social force and great communicator. We, as his children, strive to imitate him and be worthy of him.

~ 7 ~

IMPROVING
CONDITIONS

BETWEEN 1945 AND 1956, there was a certain amount of industrial unrest amongst local Aramco employees, including a number of strikes. The last strike began on October 1, 1956, the very day that I started my annual leave that year. The strikes had, in the opinion of most locals at the time, a largely successful outcome: they generated a better salary structure and improved living standards, as evidenced by the introduction of the home ownership program; better developed community services and facilities; and improved access to health centers. However, these benefits came at a cost and most of the strikes' instigators paid a heavy personal price, some even winding up in prison for a while.

The two most significant strikes occurred in 1953 and 1956, and were jointly organized by native Saudis and Arab expatriates. In 1953, a labor committee was formed to petition for better working conditions for Saudis and its members primarily wanted to be recognized as legitimate representatives of Aramco's workforce (something like a trade union). Members of this committee included seven Saudis who had previously been sent to study in the United States or in Lebanon. Their chairman was a man named Abdul Aziz Al-Sunaid, who had joined Aramco in 1949 as a teacher's assistant and quickly became known for his socialist views. While attending summer school at the American University of Beirut, he was exposed to Arab leftist ideologies, going on to enlist the support of some sympathetic Palestinian workers to create the labor committee.

Al-Sunaid and his committee presented their demands to both Aramco and the Saudi Arabian government. As a result, a government commission was set up to examine the working conditions at Aramco. The workers' committee refused to deal with the commission until it received formal recognition. In response, the whole workers' committee was arrested on October 15, 1953 and taken to jail in Hofuf. They became popular heroes overnight for standing up to the commission and a strike by the other Aramco Arab workers (about 13,000 in all) then commenced, lasting about two weeks.

That first labor strike of 1953 made something of an impression on me. I was still very young, and the strike did not actually disrupt my daily life too much, but it was certainly the talk of the town. Due to my lack of knowledge and experience, I could not know how much the wider company operations were disrupted or affected. However, I was much more aware of the concern in the Al-Khobar communities: while the residents did not know all the reasons for the strike, there was a general feeling that it would inevitably lead to improvements in employees' living conditions and standards. I did participate in the strike — I had no choice — but most colleagues just stayed at home.

All of the announcements and calls to action were in Arabic, and I gained some awareness of what was going on through reading those publications. In my opinion, looking back on it, the strike came at a most appropriate time: It was desirable and necessary because Saudi living conditions, safety at work and the overall conditions of the workers were all of very poor standards. After a strike in 1947, the government had adopted new labor policies mandating an eight-hour workday and a six-day working week, but Aramco, as a foreign company, still did not do enough to make life comfortable for the locals. I also feel that Aramco at that time may have taken advantage of the government's lack of experience and knowledge about business or industrial procedures. They seemed to do whatever they wanted, and much of that as cheaply as possible. Consequently, a strike became an important vehicle for raising awareness of the many improvements needed in the working and living conditions of the company's local employees.

I think the strike lasted about 20 days in the end, with at least 50 people winding up in custody. Many of these individuals were sent to Al-Hasa, where there was a prison that had been maintained and run by the Ottomans before King Abdul Aziz Al-Saud took the region back from the Turks. It was known as the *sejin al abied*, or the "prison of slaves." Former inmates who are still alive today will tell you they remember 15 or 16 of them having their feet constrained in a wooden column on the floor to restrict their movement. Their hands were also chained so they could not do anything. The only time they were released was to go to the toilet. Even if you got sick and complained that you needed some medicine, they kept you there, reminding you that you were being punished, and not there for a comfortable or good life.

Both the Saudi government and the regional governor of Dammam were tough and unsympathetic towards the strikers. When the governor was appointed to manage the Labor Office, he did not improve the situation very much. However, the new King Saud, who assumed the throne in 1953, was more receptive to change and encouraged labor hearings in the area. He assigned somebody by the name of Abdul Aziz Al-Mu'amar, a prominent man from Taif, as the head of the Labor Office. He was much more helpful. He listened to the complaints and then asked Aramco to listen to the strikers, requesting the company to do whatever it could to improve their living standards.

The company's representatives were not the most cooperative, holding similar attitudes to those of the governor. After Mu'amar took over at the Labor Office, it was rumored they tried to discredit him. The following story was spread around the community at that time and may or may not be true. Aramco had a Sudanese employee who used to run one of the company's magazines or newspapers at that time. He was sent to Lebanon and, while there, printed some kind of paper to be distributed to all Aramco employees detailing what the labor committee's demands were. Apparently, he had also included in the publication an image of the Soviet hammer-and-sickle symbol, with the (alleged) intention of scaring the Saudi government into thinking the strikers were communists.

These documents were discovered in his briefcase when he returned to Aramco. Although he had written things that made the Saudi government look bad, there was also suspicion locally that Aramco may have been somewhat complicit because he was an employee who worked for the company as a writer. When this all became public, it seriously concerned King Saud. He took Mu'amar into custody in Al-Hasa with the rest of the strikers, fearing that they were now asking not only for improved conditions but also for a change in government and society with a view to adopting a communist system. Thus, Aramco was let off the hook for a short time.

A delegation of workers then travelled to Lebanon, where they spoke to Kamal Jumblatt, the prominent Druze leader and politician (and father of Walid), who was a good friend of King Saud. They asked him to convince the king that the publication was a fabrication and to advocate for Mu'amar and stress his status as an honorable man from a good family with a previously spotless reputation. They stressed that Mu'amar had merely been trying to calm the company's employees in order to get them back to work, while at the same time pursuing Aramco to improve their conditions. Jumblatt did indeed intervene on their behalf, with the result that Mu'amar was released from prison.

The Saudi government held Aramco responsible for the situation and deported the Sudanese employee. The government went on to deport both the strike leaders and many of the foreign workers who had been involved.

Aramco was then obliged to bring about the further improvement of conditions for its local employees, developments which included pay raises, better working conditions and the release of the other workers arrested during the strike.

The results of the strike were positive. Working conditions were significantly improved generally for all employees and a new labor law was passed. I believe that Aramco assisted in preparing the paperwork, but the drafting was mainly done by young employees selected by the Labor Office — some of the best-educated Saudis at the time were asked to design the law. It was expected that Aramco would implement the law as an example for others to follow. Years later, I asked Aramco's General Counsel, Bill Owen, about this process and he confirmed that Aramco did help, but the bulk of the work had been done by these specially selected young Saudis.

The changes that were implemented included improved transportation (the open trucks were no longer to be used) and better housing. The home ownership program was established, and schools started to be built in local communities. These new schools attracted a better caliber of employee to come into the area and work for Aramco. In my opinion, that strike was an eye-opener and caused Aramco to become much better at listening to its workforce.

There was no noticeable bitterness from the Americans afterwards; most of those I dealt with were kind and supportive and appeared to have no strong feelings either for or against the issues. My boss never discussed these events with me. He saw it as the responsibility of the company's Industrial Relations department and felt that our only concern was to get our job done, training staff and so on. A book was published soon after the events, but it was not allowed into Saudi Arabia at the time. I don't know if it is still available, but it gave a brief account of how the strike started, who got hurt, what was achieved, and what the working conditions were like. People had not previously been given much opportunity to influence the improvement of their living standards, so the strike brought a lot of comfort to them and generated many important changes in Aramco and, subsequently, the Kingdom as a whole.

As a youngster, when I had been caught playing around in class with my friend, I was given three days' suspension without pay. The new labor law changed this so that warnings should first be given before any punitive action was taken. The new system required multiple warnings: a first, a second and then a third and final warning, leading to dismissal. This was a more modern, logical and practical approach.

~ 8 ~

PERSONNEL ISSUES

I CONTINUED WORKING FOR Mr. Don Richards in the Training Division until late 1955. By that point, I had been promoted to the lofty position of Head Clerk. The following year, however, I was transferred to the Personnel Department to gain experience as an administrative aide for a couple of years. That transition saw me become a Grade 6 employee — a significant change for me as I progressed from being just a general employee to an intermediate staff level.

In 1956, I was also asked by the Principal of the Industrial Training Center to teach Arabic at night as part of a campaign against illiteracy in the old Saudi camp. My 30 or so students were older, mostly over 50 years of age, and learning to read was a challenge for many of them. However, there were also many who persevered with studying, at least until they had finished the first year. It was a rewarding experience for me to be teaching those mature men and I particularly admired their enthusiasm, punctuality and eagerness to regularly attend their classes. I recall that Abdullah Al-Thumairi became the school principal while I was there.

In Personnel, one of my first surprising discoveries was that the company workforce then included about 35 different nationalities, mostly from the countries closest to the Kingdom's borders. So many years later, we are still somewhat indebted to those who contributed their time and talent to help build the young Saudi Arabia. Unfortunately, I feel they do not often receive an appropriate acknowledgement for their contributions.

Throughout my time in Personnel I was mentored by a number of key advisors, including Ramzi Madany, Mohammed Sabri, Ahmed Jumah and Bill Bowman. They invested considerable time ensuring I was exposed to the overall scope of this field, encouraging me to familiarize myself with many different tasks and responsibilities in the process. Consequently, I gained valuable experience in employee relations, labor relations, and counseling techniques. Firm foundational knowledge and skills meant that, toward the end of 1959, I was ready for promotion to the full role of Personnel Counselor. This was a new position that would require me to go out of the Kingdom on a number of occasions to receive further training.

In the Kingdom today, training is seen as crucial to developing a Saudi workforce skilled enough to replace expat employees. When I joined Personnel, every key position from unit level upwards was held by an American. As a Personnel Counselor, handling the work performance of employees, I dealt with the Americans in unit-level positions on a daily basis. They had been carefully selected and, with both personal issues and work-related problems, I found them to be well experienced and knowledgeable. None of them held a university degree, but many had a technical diploma and extensive experience in technical work, including carpentry, welding, office machinery, printing, mechanics and domestic appliance maintenance.

At first, the Saudis did not generally possess these kinds of skills, but they took their training and work seriously, and in the meantime their labor was complemented by the necessary skill sets supplied by Indians, Pakistanis, Yemenis, Somalis and Italians. I was impressed with the approach of the Italians because they were all anxious to return to their home country after they had passed on the required skills. Many of them accomplished this goal and left. Unfortunately, some of the others lacked enthusiasm to develop the young Saudis, being more concerned for their own prospects.

All of the foremen I dealt with back then were Americans, who were keen to ensure their children received the best education possible, especially as they had not been privileged enough to access the same opportunities when they were growing up. Working for Aramco meant they were able to offer their children more. Over the years, I have been so happy to see and observe many of the children of those American foremen achieve high levels of professional education, some becoming doctors, engineers and lawyers. I am still in touch with some of their children and I am very proud of their successes and achievements in life.

AN INCIDENT INVOLVING SHOES

One particular incident sticks in my mind that illustrates the kinds of daily tasks we sometimes had to deal with in Personnel. On this day, Khalil Younis, a foreman in Maintenance, called and informed me that he and a crew of workers had arrived at the home of Mr. Ned Scardino (District Manager of Dhahran) to do some repair work in one of the bathrooms. However, the lady of the house refused to allow the workers access through the house unless they took off their shoes. I told him to remove his employees from the site while I discussed the matter with Mr. Scardino.

Mr. Scardino was known as a strong proponent of site safety and, when I met with him, I reminded him of this in the context of his wife refusing entry to the maintenance team unless they removed their shoes. He approved of my action in temporarily standing down the team and then tasked me to find a solution. As a result of that incident, we started laying down a plastic covering for workers to walk on from the nearest entrance to any worksite inside a house. This meant there was no longer a need for them to remove their safety shoes. Mr. Scardino was most happy with the outcome.

> *In the mid-1950s, Ali and I both transferred from other company departments to work within the Personnel Department for employees. We were based in the old Dhahran District area. Ali's job was with the Personnel Administration/Services Group, while I was with the Personnel Advisory/Counseling Group, but we shared the same supervisor. Our work relationship continued over the years and eventually developed into a real long-lasting friendship, continuing to this day.*
>
> **AHMED AL-HAZZA**

A VISIT TO EXXON

In 1958, Mustafa Abu Ahmed and I were selected to spend a month on a tour of Exxon facilities in the United States to examine their approaches to the management of Human Resources. Being my first trip to America, it was certainly an eye-opener! We flew from Dhahran via Amsterdam and Shannon airports before finally landing at LaGuardia Airport in New York. It was a very long and tiresome trip, taking us more than 20 hours of flying time.

We joined up with about 30 other human resources staff, all from Exxon affiliates elsewhere around the world. Observing Exxon's HR operations throughout the country proved quite a revelation, greatly enhancing our professional knowledge of, and approaches to, the wider management of HR. A bonus for me was discovering how to avoid unnecessarily duplicating paperwork!

One of the areas we observed during our visit was the influence and strength of the labor unions in a variety of workplaces across the United States. Some union representatives were clearly concerned when they discovered we were from overseas. The foremen seemed to be under the impression that we were visiting the country in order to discover better ways and means to suppress and control the workforces in our own companies.

Many of the HR organizational structures we observed in Exxon were completely different from the way Aramco organized its HR in the Kingdom. Aramco had much more limited resources available, so its HR structure had been specifically established to manage manpower resources to meet operational needs. However, it seemed to us that this system actually allowed Aramco more freedom to run its own business effectively without the need for, or interference by, labor unions.

Overall, the trip gave us a much better understanding of the role of HR within an oil company. We were particularly impressed with the quality of Exxon's personnel — they were all well-educated and received a high level of ongoing relevant training, making them generally better prepared for their tasks than we were with only our limited work experience behind us.

I was thrilled by the whole program, including the many other activities planned to enhance our visit. The trip had allowed me some valuable insights into the American culture of the late 1950s.

A visit to Houston was one of the special aspects of the program, but our group was surprised to find there that certain kinds of refreshment were not available in local restaurants. Apparently, if you wanted such refreshments with your meals, it was a requirement to join a club in one of the hotels. I recall being invited to a dinner outside of our hotel in a restaurant on the outskirts of Houston. Having previously bought their refreshments from the club located in the Sheraton Hotel (where we were staying), members of our group had to ignominiously carry them to the dinner in so-called "brown bags," making us all feel as if we were doing something rather underhanded!

LOCAL BUSINESSES DEVELOPING FROM ARAMCO CONNECTIONS

There are many examples of successful Saudi businessmen who originally started their careers with Aramco. I first met a number of them while I was assigned to the Personnel Department, and I continued to follow and admire their ongoing achievements. At that time, Aramco approved and allowed a leave of absence of six months to encourage Saudis to explore their ideas for new business ventures. Many took advantage of this and were very successful, but there were some who returned to work for the company when their leave expired.

Abdullah Fouad is a businessman I greatly respect, and he was well-known for his infectious enthusiasm. He started at Aramco as an office boy when he was 16 years old, on one riyal per day. He worked hard at improving his skills and eventually was assigned to the Ras Tanura Personnel Office. In mid-1947, he resigned from the company to work as a contractor, taking on several small assignments and making some remarkable profits. In 1948, Abdullah joined with Suliman Al-Ollayan and a few other contractors to build the oil pipeline from the Eastern Province to Lebanon. Subsequently, he was contracted to construct several schools for Aramco in Al-Khobar, Dammam and Ras Tanura (Rahimah).

In the latter part of his life, Abdullah Fouad went into partnership with his friend Ali bin Abdullah Al-Tamimi. They became involved in prospect investments and major owners of several banks, hotels and supermarkets, including the well-known Tamimi-Safeway, and other food and entertainment outlets. Abdullah also personally assisted some other Saudis in starting their own companies in plastic packaging and paper products. In early 1980, his 310-bed hospital was opened in Dammam.

Abdullah Fouad's business legacy did not come without challenges. In the 1980s, the economic situation in the Gulf area caused foreign banks in Bahrain to increase pressure to reconcile accounts quickly, and Abdullah was forced to sell most of his businesses in order to meet his commitments. However, he reinvented himself and became very much engaged in the development of electronics and IT in the Kingdom. With his aggressive business acumen, he quickly revived his status. We were very grateful for all the support he later gave us with the 2000 Saudi Aramco Expat Reunion.

Ali bin Abdullah Al-Tamimi and Suliman Al-Ollayan also began their business ventures after leaving Aramco service. Abdul Hadi Al-Qahtani started in Maintenance but stepped out to create a pipeline wrapping company. As I recall, he went to a local bank for a loan, but his request was denied, so Aramco's Local Industrial Development Group (specifically a man named Stormy Weathers), intervened and persuaded the bank to release the loan conditional on it being guaranteed by Aramco.

Hassan Abdul Karim Al-Qahtani originally worked in Exploration but was supported to start his own business after exhibiting attributes of good leadership. Ahmed Al-Gosaibi left his post in Aramco Personnel to join his father in creating a money exchange business in Al-Khobar and Aramco bought riyals from them to run its operations, notably to pay the salaries of its employees. Abdul Rahman Al-Saeed and Mohammed Al-Arfaj were contracted to bring fruit and vegetables from Hofuf and the Aramco farm in Al-Kharj, near Riyadh.

Having so long admired their tenacity and enthusiasm in the business world, I was thrilled when some of these men offered sponsorships for the first Saudi Aramco Expatriate Reunion, held in March 2000. Those generous souls included Abdul Aziz Al-Turki, Abdullah Rushaid and Abdul Aziz Al-Turaiki. I must particularly mention Ali bin Abdullah Al-Tamimi, who assisted by providing all the bus transportation needs for the duration of this first Saudi Arabia reunion event.

SOFT DRINKS

The 1950s was the era when the soft drink became popular in Saudi Arabia. My family would sometimes be sent *bebsi cola* from Bahrain in return for sending our friends lemons and dates. Aramco initially imported cola products for its employees and their families, but eventually it built a small manufacturing plant in the Dhahran camp. It later sold the plant to the local Al-Gosaibi family for the nominal amount of one dollar. Abdul Aziz Al-Gosaibi then negotiated a deal with the main Pepsi-Cola company in New York to develop an expanded facility in Al-Khobar.

Another new drinks manufacturing plant was opened in Al-Khobar in 1959 by Mohammed Al-Saeed, one of the businessmen who previously helped the company deliver fruit and vegetables from the Aramco farms. Here, "sugar cola" was produced in a variety of flavors such as orange, lemon, grape and ginger. This plant was eventually forced to close for commercial reasons. I believe the product was not so popular and, like many others, its potential market had not been properly researched in advance. Also, at that time, marketing strate-gies were not taken very seriously. I remember attending a petroleum conference for Aramco in 1963 in Beirut, where Sheikh Abdullah Al-Turaiki was laughed at by other businessmen when he suggested that oil products should be marketed to the end-users wherever they were. These days, Saudi Aramco has offices all over the world to enable more effective marketing and sales of its products.

In the early 1960s, another soft drink plant began operating in Dammam, owned by the Kaki family who developed a product known as "Kaki Cola". When cola first became popular, I recall that it was served in Arabic coffee cups so several people could share a bottle at the same time!

Aramco gave away the running of a number of its own service facilities to local businesspeople. The ice-cream plant was passed to Abdullah Al-Matrood, as well as a laundry facility situated at the Saudi Community Camp (the area now occupied by the King Fahd University of Petroleum and Minerals). Al-Matrood later expanded the ice-cream plant to handle a variety of other dairy products. Aramco continued to provide technical assistance to these businesses to ensure they were properly run and retained the correct standards of hygiene and maintenance. In a few instances, Aramco even hired consultants to ensure the plants were managed efficiently. For many years, the company continued regular inspections of these plants, especially those from which it sourced products for its own employees' consumption.

1

2

1 This is now a popular
   location on the
   Corniche for visitors
   to Al-Khobar.

2 Writing a book provides
   opportunity for some
   family portraits.

1

1 Fishing nets and dhows, Darin Island, Eastern Province. *Dorothy Miller Collection*

2 Aerial view of Al-Khobar, 1950.

3 Aramco's General Camp around the time when my father was held there in custody.

4 A traditional *barasti* dwelling from Darin Island, Eastern Province, 1974. *Dorothy Miller Collection*

3

4

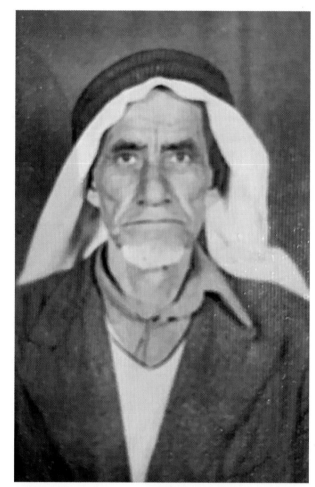

1 A rare image of my
   father Mohammed
   Ali Al-Baluchi.

2 My elder brother,
   Abdul Rahman

3 My brother Jassim

1

2

3

4

4 This photo of me is from around the time I started work at Aramco. It was published in 1974 as part of an article in the *Arabian Sun* newspaper about I.D. cards. My badge number was 49349.

5 An Arabic class in progress in Aramco's Jebel School, 1947–8. I enrolled as a part-time student in 1947 and remember this classroom and the teacher, Mr. Fahmi Basrawi.

5

1 Aramco's Advanced
Clerical Training
Center, 1950.

2 Meeting 103-year-old
retiree Johnnie Merritt
in Houston, 2018. She
knew me in Dhahran
in the late 1940s and
said she recalled me
as "a little office boy,
carrying papers and
things around and
running errands." She
arrived in Dhahran
as Johnnie Rusher in
1948, working first in
the Steno Pool, then
moving to Engineering,
Personnel and
Government Relations.

3 At work with
Don Richards.

4 As a young man in
Western-style clothing.

1

2

3

4

1

2

3

4

1 Offering hospitality is very important to me. On this occasion, my sons were present with my neighbor and Aramco CEO Abdullah Jumah.

2 A portrait of me from 1962.

3 With Khalil Younis in 1992, the foreman who handled the "shoes incident."

4 At an Aramco exhibit with Mustafa Abu Ahmed, my traveling companion on the 1958 Exxon trip.

5

6

7

5 With my colleagues in Personnel, 1956.

6 Visiting with Nancy Washburne and her children.

7 Dr. Karl Hartzell, Dean of Bucknell University, and his dear family.

8 The last time I met with Mrs. Elli Beckley was in the United States at her home, featured here with her son Pete and his family. It was just two weeks before she passed away.

8

1

2

1 With me are: standing (L to R) Helen Dunn, Lois Bonner (with Corky the dog), Genevieve Monego, me, Connie and Rebecca Monego, Jess Ann Dunn. Seated: Mahlon Dunn, Jed Monego, Thomas Monego and Pepper the dog.

2 Saying farewell to summer school students at Lewisburg bus station after the program.

3 Bucknell University Summer Program students, June 1960.

4 Re-visiting Peirce College in 1986 to participate in the 125th anniversary celebrations (I am on the far right).

5 Ahmed Al-Hazza and me at graduation.

4

5

6

6 Receiving some
personal attention from
the Dean of Peirce.

7 Being able to travel to
the United States for my
education and training
was always an exciting
adventure! This was
taken on a visit to
New York City.

1

2

1 My role at International House involved welcoming students. Here I am with some visiting Sudanese students, in 1961.

2 Representing Aramco at the 1963 Oil Conference in Beirut, speaking with Sheikh Abdul Aziz Al-Mani' (in the middle).

~ 9 ~

COLLEGE CONNECTIONS

IN THE SPRING of 1960, I was excited and proud to be one of the 10 young Saudis selected to go overseas for further education. It was even announced in the weekly Aramco newspaper, *Sun and Flare*.

Before I could travel, I had to visit the American Consulate General in Dhahran to obtain a visa for the United States. Mr. Abdul Rahman Bubshait was working at the front desk. He took all the required documents from me and, in only four hours, I received the visa. Comparing that with the present situation, how drastically things have changed! Since the events of September 11, 2001, neither the Consul General nor the Ambassador has any influence over the issuance of visas, the responsibility resting solely with the Secretary of Homeland Security. And now, too, we have to run the gauntlet of being processed through United States Immigration and Customs! In many ways, it was a much easier and better time back then.

I recall being given a topcoat to wear while abroad by Mr. Bill McGovern, a Personnel Advisor. That topcoat was certainly well-used and much appreciated during the winter season! It was a very kind gesture.

I started my studies by attending a summer orientation program at Bucknell University in Lewisburg, Pennsylvania, a program which included both industrial visits to companies such as Hershey and the Corning Glass Company, and invaluable input about American culture and customs. Once this introductory course was completed, I progressed to attend the Peirce School of Business Administration (now Peirce College) in Philadelphia, initially for one year.

From the very beginning, I viewed my schooling and training experiences in the United States and elsewhere in the world as providing me with precious opportunities to develop what would often go on to become long-lasting and special friendships. As I continued to attend conferences and seminars overseas, and while I was still young and able to travel comfortably, I would use every occasion to visit and catch up with my friends. Unfortunately, age is now catching up with me, and I am sad that I cannot make my visits as frequently as I used to. In my younger days, I could travel to many different parts of America over a 15-day period. Once I even passed through 10 airports in one trip! I enjoyed being able to meet a friend for breakfast in one place, eat lunch with a different dear friend somewhere else, and then share dinner with a friend in yet another location.

During my early stays in the States, I enjoyed the experience of going to different churches on Sundays. I feel that being exposed to different kinds of religion and religious practices brought me to an understanding that we are all fundamentally the same and we all believe in the one God. At the Methodist church in Philadelphia, I attended the youth sessions which were held on Sunday afternoons. Each week, the chair would introduce invited speakers to share from their different fields of expertise such as drugs education, health issues or history, and I found these very interesting and rewarding sessions. By attending the various churches, I was also able to make many new friends.

I know there were those who were concerned about me doing this, as they were afraid that I might convert to Christianity. I think it just made me generally more tolerant and open-minded.

The Bowen family introduced me to their parents in Willow Grove, Pennsylvania, with whom I stayed in touch until they both passed away. It became a special tradition that, whenever I visited the family, they would make me a delicious apple pie, a dish I still enjoy to this day.

Another family which I got to know well was the Hartzells.

RICHARD HARTZELL WAS A CHILD WHEN ALI VISITED HIS FAMILY HOME AS A "FOREIGN STUDENT"

My father, Karl. D. Hartzell, was Dean of Bucknell University at the time when Ali was a "foreign student" there. The university had set up a program to help international students from different countries learn about America, its culture, ways of living, language, manners and dress. The program was run by my mother, Anne Hartzell.

Ali was one of the students who represented Saudi Arabia in this program. There were several events and "classes" held for these foreign students at our private home in Lewisburg, Pennsylvania. As director of this program, my mother came to know all of the students quite well, including Ali, and the others in my family did as well.

Ali was the quintessence of politeness and elegance, quiet energy and intelligence, sincerely interested in learning all he could about America, and being a wonderful friend of all who came to know him. He had a ready smile and gentle sense of humor, and his warm affection for my mother and our family reflected our great fondness for him. He was a very dear and kind man.

My mother's responsibilities were to instruct the foreign students in American ways of living, interacting with others, polite behavior between men and women, table manners, ways of speaking, etc. It was as if she were training these lovely young people as her own children who needed her guidance, and she gave it to them with patience and kindness as any mother would have. Ali came to refer to her — both [with] the other students and [with] her and her family directly — as "Mother Hartzell." It was a beautiful indicator of his gratitude toward her as well as his genuine affection for her and our family.

After the completion of only one year studying in the United States, my Aramco boss tried to negotiate my return to the Kingdom because he had a position waiting to be filled. I was more interested in continuing my schooling in America, in order to complete my diploma. I decided to write a letter to Paul Arnot, the General Manager of Oil Operations, for whom I had previously handled a few grievance cases during my tenure as a Personnel Advisor. At the time, he had been very supportive of my work. In the letter, I requested his assistance in persuading the Saudi Development Committee to let me finish my schooling.

A few years later, after he had retired, the then Secretary of the Dhahran Saudi Development Committee shared with me how that story had evolved. Apparently Arnot had called Frank Jungers, who was then the Chair of the Saudi Development Committee, expressing his desire to attend the next meeting. At the meeting, Mr. Jungers gave him the floor. Arnot said he only had one simple request of the committee: that they extend Ali Baluchi's stay in the United States. Arnot testified that, from his own experience, I was a good employee and he personally considered me an asset to Aramco, believing that extending my study time would only benefit the company in the long run. As he was Head of Operations, they could hardly deny his request!

I met Paul Arnot again many years later, and I was glad of the opportunity to express my appreciation for his support. His expressions were always so inscrutable that it was difficult to tell how he was feeling; he was well-known for looking down at your shoes all the time he was holding a conversation with you — a practice I found most disconcerting!

INTERNATIONAL FRIENDSHIPS

Studying a long way from home can have its challenges, especially if one gets sick. In 1961, while visiting a family I had become close to, I developed a severe pain. The host family tried to care for me but the pain continued. Eventually my friend Ahmed Al-Hazza took me to the nearest clinic, where the doctor discovered I had a small kidney stone. The doctor gave me shots and told me I would be referred to the Hahnemann Hospital in Philadelphia for further treatment.

Two weeks later, I reported to the hospital and saw a specialist from Boston. After a few hours' wait, I was operated on and the stone was removed. I spent a few days in the hospital. Many of my friends came to visit me while I recovered and the hospital staff cared for me.

One of my classmates, my dear friend Adelaide "Addie" Hudson, visited me regularly at the hospital. Addie was a lovely person and very kind to me during my early college years, staying in touch until my graduation in June 1962 — in fact, all the time I lived in Philadelphia. From my hospital bed, I dictated to her many messages and letters for my friends, and notes and assignments for some of my teachers.

Adelaide's kind attention kept me up to date with all my classes and prevented me from falling behind with any coursework. My professors were also very happy that I communicated regularly with them. I was thus able, through the help of my dear friend, to successfully conclude the term.

SANDRA ATKINSON VALUES A FRIENDSHIP
BEGUN IN BUSINESS SCHOOL

In the fall of 1960, while attending the Peirce Business School in Philadelphia, I encountered Ali and several of his fellow workers from Aramco who were all living in a nearby apartment. Several of my friends became friends with them and now all share many pleasant memories of our times together. Once we finished our time at Peirce, Joyce, Penny, Addie and I still remained in contact with Ali.

As an international student, I was fortunate enough to be invited to attend an all-Arab student convention in Minnesota in July 1961. Even though we all had some kind of Arab ethnicity, I discovered this large body of students came from a wide variety of backgrounds, some very different to my own, especially with regard to some of their political beliefs and cultural practices. Unfortunately, on the bus trip home from the convention, my suitcase went missing, and it took me a while to get myself organized again. I guess I must have failed to tip a porter at the bus terminal! Dr. Hartzell, the Dean of Bucknell University, kindly came to my rescue with his children.

In 1962, I was elected Vice President of the Arab Students' Council in Pennsylvania. Being the representative of all the Arab students from overseas then attending colleges in Philadelphia brought certain privileges, including an invitation to attend the city's annual Grand New Year Dance. This turned out to be a very special occasion, where I met many influential business leaders and important figures from the local communities.

On another occasion, I was asked to represent my fellow international students by attending the annual breakfast held by the city mayors of Pennsylvania. I can still remember the Mayor of Philadelphia introducing me to the illustrious gathering as "a young man from Saudi Arabia attending Peirce College in Philadelphia." I was so very proud to be representing my country in that way.

While living in Philadelphia and attending the Peirce School, my growing interest in getting to know others from around the world also prompted me to become Vice Chairman of the International House Council for a year. I then took on the role of Chairman of the International Student Organization.

Because of my level of commitment to representing my country as a foreign student, I was invited by one of the college publications at Peirce to submit an article entitled "Why Have Friendships?" I was pleased to oblige them.

The following is the text of the original article, included here because I feel it illustrates how many of my current convictions were already quite firmly formulated by this time.

WHY HAVE FRIENDSHIPS?

*What is Friendship? Webster's New College Dictionary
defines its meaning: "State of being friends, friendly
attachment; friendliness; amity." It is possible to achieve
a peaceful world by a mutual and constructive friendship
among all peoples. I believe there is no better investment
than having friends. Since my departure from my homeland,
Saudi Arabia, I have aimed for two objectives. First, to seek
more knowledge, and second, to create friendship for the
betterment of all.*

*I realize the ultimate goal of a foreign student coming to
the Unites States is education, but he is still obligated to his
people to inspire good will among Americans. For example,
the role expected of an Arab student in the US is to establish
stronger ties with the American people through better mutual
understanding and to disseminate true information about
the Arab people, their culture, history, ideas and aspirations.
He is to promote better understanding and closer relations
in the various students' organizations, such as The National
Student Association and All-African Student Union.*

*The Cultural Program Committee of Peirce is contacting
all foreign representatives in the US to provide us with
information so that it may be placed in the library for
the students' use. The purpose of this project is to get the
students acquainted with all parts of the world and people
from every walk of life to achieve a true understanding and
friendship.*

ALI M. BALUCHI, CHAIRMAN CULTURAL PROGRAM

COMMITTEE, PEIRCE SCHOOL

Later, I received a different kind of invitation — this time from a major TV station! They wanted me to participate with other international students in recording a discussion about communism and how destructive it could be to young people. The program's aim was to encourage American youth to stand together to control the spread and influence of the evil ideology. Once aired, the program was very well-received; some of my friends in Los Angeles saw it when it was broadcast.

Being on the TV program brought further invitations for speaking engagements at a variety of groups. These were mostly interested in hearing about Saudi Arabia. I was so proud of my heritage. Aramco Public Relations in Houston were very supportive and sent me some useful information to share in my presentations. I was rather surprised to discover that many in my audiences did not even know the location of Saudi Arabia on the global map! I made sure to redress that lack of knowledge!

At the other end of the spectrum, I also had a somewhat thought-provoking experience in Philadelphia. While walking near City Hall with some fellow students, we stumbled upon a group of three young kids, who turned out to be homeless. We invited them to our apartment to eat and shelter. We treated them as if they were royal guests, sharing our very best Saudi hospitality!

When we later returned from college, we discovered that the homeless children and a few other things, including some cash, were missing from the apartment. A laundromat owner near the apartment had seen our guests walking out of the back door. It seemed the three we had treated as guests returned our kindness by becoming thieves!

At a later date, my apartment partner, Ahmed Al-Hazza, and his friend Abdullah Ghanim happened to bump into one of the perpetrators and insisted on the return of all they had taken. They even accompanied the kids back to their hideout, where they were able to discover and retrieve some of the stolen items, including my alarm clock!

Because the apartment we leased was close to Peirce School, we regularly invited our classmates, and I can thankfully say we never experienced any problems with them. In fact, many of them stayed in touch with us for some time after leaving college, which we greatly appreciated and cherished.

One evening, my friend Ahmed Al-Hazza and I decided to throw a special party for all our friends in Philadelphia. At the end of the evening, he decided to drive a friend back to their home outside of the city. On the way, he somehow managed to drive straight through four red lights, assuming it was okay to do so at that time of night if there were no traffic police around. Unfortunately, a policeman was waiting for him at the last set of lights and he was stopped. When he was asked to account for why he was jumping the lights, Ahmed endeavored to claim that he was a new foreign student with little English and had not yet learned all the road rules.

The policeman was obviously suspicious of the English Ahmed could speak, so asked to see his ID. When he saw that Ahmed was from Saudi Arabia, he told him that if he continued to jump red lights as he had on this particular evening, the punishment would be as severe as having his hand cut off! As it was, Ahmed wound up with a 10-dollar traffic violation.

Another memorable occasion occurred after we had been given advance notice of an impending visit from a certain Mr. O'Grady. He was one of Aramco's training advisors at that time. Ahmed Al-Hazza and I were so excited about his visit that we undertook a frugal diet for several weeks in advance so we could save enough money to take him to dinner at the popular (but expensive by student standards) Bookbinder's restaurant. Our dinner and evening with Mr. O'Grady went well, and Ahmed and I were both satisfied that it had been a most enjoyable visit for all concerned.

A few weeks later, however, we received a letter from Mr. O'Grady informing us that he was decreasing our living allowance from 260 to 210 dollars a month. He obviously thought we were living too well and had too much money if we could afford to eat at such restaurants! We were quite dismayed! I tried looking for a part-time job in Philadelphia to make up the difference, but I was unsuccessful, largely due to labor union regulations about employing foreign students.

During my next visit to Saudi Arabia, I discussed the matter with my father. He agreed to make up the 50-dollar difference each month. I learned a lesson — we went out of our way to be nice to Mr. O'Grady, but it backfired and ended poorly for us!

All too soon it was September 1962 and time to return to work in Saudi Arabia. Once home, I was to be assigned to the position of Personnel Advisor.

LONG-TERM FRIEND AND COLLEAGUE AHMED AL-HAZZA RECALLS THE JOYS OF BEING COLLEGE ROOMMATES

Ali and I were both sent to the same junior college in America, where we were roommates for almost two years. We had a third person also sharing the flat with us.

We agreed we would cook some of our meals in the flat and that we would rotate the chores among ourselves every month (one person would cook, one would clean the flat and one would purchase the groceries and clean the plates).

Ali hates washing dishes! During Ali's turn to clean the plates, myself and the other person tried to tease and aggravate him: for one of the meals, we went out of our way to use as many plates as possible. Ali screamed and he almost hit the ceiling! He went on to surprise us on another day by setting the table with paper plates. We refused to use the paper plates, so Ali's plan failed, making Ali one unhappy camper.

NANCY WASHBURNE EXTENDED AN INVITATION TO THANKSGIVING DINNER

My husband came home from his bowling club one November night with a huge Thanksgiving turkey he had won as a prize. I tried to think of what to do with it since we had no freezer then and lived nowhere near our families. I called my former Dean of Women at Penn and asked her if she knew who was from far away and stuck close to the college on Thanksgiving. She told me about some foreign students whom she believed nobody had invited to share the holiday. She said that if I wanted to bless some young people who couldn't afford to fly home and some Arab students who were new to Philadelphia and had no idea about Thanksgiving, I would spare them the pain of being left out. So, I asked her to give me their names.

I love to cook but had never previously met any Arabs, and she told me they had some dietary constraints. I studied fast but the constraints didn't present any problems — Thanksgiving has so many food delights to choose from.

Along came several students (all male, including Ali) and we had a huge dinner with eight vegetables and endless food. Our guests were totally absorbed with our children (we had two young toddler daughters), having missed their sisters and cousins back home, and the girls were delighted at all the attention. It was a very enjoyable day.

After this we had Arabic weekends for years, especially with Ali — and he brought more and more of his Saudi friends. Despite living in a very quiet small town, we had wonderful enjoyable dinners together, learning how these friends lived and what they celebrated, exchanging all sorts of ideas on a diversity of subjects.

I remember going with Ali to our big open market in the old city. Here we taught each other culinary things and talked about the customs of Saudi families and how they raised their children compared to American ways and customs. I recall watching American kids jumping on and hugging the Arab men. Sometimes they brought their festive clothes so we could see how Arabs dressed up. They faced [Makkah] and showed my son how to pray and often talked about believing in God and proper behaviors. The fact I own a Quran at first surprised them. But being a librarian at heart, I had Bibles too. My kids were affected wonderfully by exposure to these friends from different cultures.

~ 10 ~

CONSOLIDATING EXPERIENCE, 1962-1965

UPON MY RETURN to Dhahran, I made it a priority to rekindle my sporting interests and was quickly elected as Secretary of Al-Etihad Sports Club in Al-Khobar. I subsequently became Vice President of Al-Shu'alah Sports and Cultural Club.

Returning to work at Aramco headquarters, I held a number of different positions in Personnel before being transferred to the Labor Relations Division of Industrial Relations. There my new role was designated as 'Labor Relations Representative'.

This assignment was a particularly exciting one for a young man, and some busy and enjoyable years followed. My responsibilities required me to meet regularly with the various heads of the Ministry of Labor and Social Affairs, including the Minister himself. Sometimes, when we were handling labor disputes and issues of a particularly sensitive nature, we found it necessary to meet outside of the Kingdom for our deliberations. There were occasions when it felt quite personally challenging to represent the views of my American employer, Aramco, while dealing with other Saudi nationals, who came largely from similar backgrounds and circumstances to my own. At a professional level, the interests and views of the company were always paramount, but that did not prevent me from mediating with management for a fairer deal in several instances. I believe one of the attributes I brought to the position was my local cultural knowledge and insight and an ability to explain its relevance to management.

I was presented with a less appealing assignment in 1964 when I transferred to the Benefits Division to work as a Benefits Advisor. At the time, I did not consider this a good career move for me. However, I was told the assignment would be advantageous as it would introduce me to several Benefit Plans currently under consideration and development relating to the Saudi workforce, including the Retirement Plan for Saudi Arab employees. Looking back now, I am sure some valuable foundations were laid for my wider interest in retirement issues later in life.

As an aside, thinking about 1964 reminds me of the events of April 18, a sad day for the region, when a Middle East Airlines flight crash-landed into Al-Aziziyah Bay. The flight was arriving from Beirut in the early morning and it got caught in a shamal (the local name for a sandstorm). A search was conducted for the passengers, but sadly there were no survivors. The bodies of two Americans and one Saudi were never found. Those lost included Saudi twins, the sons of Mohammed Al-Dossari (a prominent Al-Khobar business-man) who were on their way home for the holidays from studying in Beirut.

Overall, I believe my assignments within Personnel opened my eyes to the many facets of company life where human values are important. Through this period, I also developed a strong conviction that each person's contribution to the workplace must be properly recognized and appreciated.

This period also provided me with other formative experiences including the opportunities to represent Aramco as part of its delegations to the Arab Petroleum Conferences of 1963 in Beirut and 1965 in Cairo. Among my fellow delegates were Hassan Munif and Ali Al-Naimi, my fellow student from Jebel School who would himself eventually become an Oil Minister for the Kingdom. My role at the conferences was as to act as an advisor to the head of the delegation, briefing him on relevant issues as required and ensuring that the concerns of the company were disseminated clearly to other attendees. Our overall mission was to represent Aramco's interests in the global arena with regard to making the right decisions for the development of the oil business.

During these conferences, many issues pertaining to oil and its marketing were discussed. Sheikh Abdullah Al-Turaiki, former Minister of Petroleum and Minerals, was a focal point. He stressed and encouraged the oil companies to go to the consumer instead of making the consumer come to them. At that time most of the world's oil delegates laughed at his ideas and suggestions. Nowadays, however, everybody is rushing to woo consumers in order to establish a market for their products. Isn't this incredible? We should not forget the way business was conducted then by the famous oil companies. Known as the "seven sisters," this dominant group included the Anglo-Iranian Oil Company (now British Petroleum); Gulf Oil (later part of Chevron); Royal Dutch Shell; Standard Oil Company of California; Standard Oil Company of New Jersey (now ExxonMobil); Standard Oil Company of New York (Socony, now ExxonMobil); and Texaco. These companies strived very hard to maintain control of the oil producing countries, driven wholly by their own interests.

Despite being something of a visionary, Sheikh Abdullah Al-Turaiki was disliked by some and made enemies. He felt the Aramco management did not always treat him with the respect he warranted, evidenced by the company's consistent rejection of his request for a home in Dhahran in order to accommodate his American wife and son, Sakhar. He later confessed this to me personally during a course I attended in Taif.

The Taif course was a program Sheikh Abdullah sponsored for specially selected employees of oil companies, with all the visiting professors being sourced from Harvard Business School. The course content focused on Marketing, Production, workplace efficiency and creating better relationships with consumers. I was very impressed by Sheikh Abdullah and his great insight into the future of the oil industry. I believe he may even have been the first Saudi Arabian Petroleum Engineer.

I got to know Turaiki's son, Sakhar, on a visit he made to Al-Khobar. At that time, I leased out part of my family compound in order to help with maintenance costs and one of my tenants was a local bank manager, living there with his family. Sakhar was a friend of that family and came to stay with them. One day, I saw this young man in the compound and asked him what he was doing there. He explained that he was staying with his friends and in the course of the conversation I discovered that he was the son of Al-Turaiki.

I believe that Sheikh Al-Turaiki did eventually come to live in Dhahran with his American wife. The company appeared to do a lot of questionable things in its early years, but it survived because it was so badly needed by the Saudi government — the government desperately required somebody to explore for, produce and sell their oil, both for themselves and for the people of Saudi Arabia. Aramco was not always very flexible: Their principal concern was to make the king happy and as long as they did that, it was perhaps questionable how much they cared about the rest. They were reluctant to allow Saudis to live in the main residential camps, claiming that King Abdul Aziz Al-Saud had instructed them to fence their residential communities and discourage non-Christians from living within the designated family compounds. In later years, I asked some key personnel in the company's Government Relations department if that was so and they denied it, saying it was a rule created by a few who were anti-Saudi.

This certainly jibed with my own experiences. Throughout my career at Aramco, I observed there were two types of Americans within the company: those who were very committed to teaching and helping the Saudis to progress, and those who resisted helping because they did not want to risk losing their own positions or status.

PROGRESS FOR SAUDIS

In the early years, any progress made through the company by educated and experienced Saudis was slow. As time passed, momentum increased, fueled by the growing range of opportunities on offer through training and broader workplace exposure. I experienced this slow progress myself for quite some time until eventually some of my American colleagues noticed the relative tardiness of my promotions.

A promotional block was often caused by the extended retention of some expatriate in order for them to attain the added benefits offered at retirement age or significant service milestones. It caused me some considerable angst when the promotions did not come as smoothly to me as I felt I deserved, and I witnessed management time and again assigning less qualified managers in my place — at times, my distress led me to feel unhappy and even ill. I have a strong sense of injustice!

Some expatriates seemed demanding and harsh when handling the nationals, but they were usually protected and held above reproach because they held crucial positions within the company. It was a tough time, especially when I was working in Personnel and handling employee discipline and grievances; I often was quite conflicted. Despite this, it is imperative not to overlook the raft of important workplace behaviors we Saudis learned from the Americans, such as the need to be punctual and meet deadlines.

There are a number of Americans from that era for whom I still retain a very great respect, including some that I worked for directly. These indomitable characters included Don Richards, Larry Crampton, Brock Powers, Les Goss, Hal Fogulquist, Dan Sullivan, Paul Arnot, Frank Jungers, Bob Luttrell, Jim Ehl, George Covey, Bill Griffin, Bob Ryrholm and Fritz Taylor. These men not only enabled Saudis to advance but made major policy changes to bring about transformation within the company and its structures. While the process still remained slow, I respected them as open-minded representatives of management, and I felt they had a realistic approach to ensuring the readiness of Saudis to assume new positions.

I can remember a particular conversation I had with Ali Al-Naimi when he was in Abqaiq on a development assignment in the mid-1960s. Ali shared with me how he was becoming increasingly uncomfortable with the length of the assignments he was given. I encouraged him to persevere, and to focus on the coming of a more promising future. Like me, his progress was slowed by an American employee the company wanted to take care of first. I think the company was not always fair to Ali. I had known Ali since we had attended the Jebel School and he was competent, knowledgeable and had become a most virtuous and likeable young man.

Many Saudi assignments were too long, and they were often characterized by simple tasks that did not give proper opportunity for learning both the required and new skills. Sometimes you can learn a lot by watching how others lead and following their example, but mentoring was not a popular concept at that time.

AHMED AL-HAZZA REFLECTS ON ASSERTIVE COMMUNICATION

In 1962, Ali and I returned from studying in the US and both got promoted at the same time to professional level jobs. This meant we progressed from our intermediate jobs to Senior Staff jobs, which meant more money and higher status. Having approved our promotions, the District Manager then took his time before visiting our office to congratulate us on the promotion and to wish us good luck for the future. Instead of being thankful when he did, Ali looked the District Manager in the eye and without any hesitation told him that the promotion was long overdue. This angered and embarrassed the manager, and he left in a hurry.

I recall another similar incident when we both went to the office of the Director of Industrial Relations to bid him farewell on his retirement. We exchanged some pleasantries and then the gentleman proceeded to enthuse over some new charts he had produced that detailed the development and progress of Saudis within the company. Ali abruptly told him the charts were useless and he had

better take them with him when he retired. What Ali
meant was that the man had not used his tenure and
position as leader to develop Saudis while he could, so the
charts meant nothing.

In response to the above incident, I reacted from frustration because I thought these plans would be very difficult to administer into practice once the proponent had retired. We had waited many years for significant changes, but none had previously materialized. When I expressed my displeasure, it was at the bad timing.

~ 11 ~

ABQAIQ,
THE FRIENDLY CITY

IN 1965, I was assigned to Abqaiq as Acting Administrator of Area Personnel for a period of five weeks, covering for Mustafa Abu Ahmed while he was on his annual vacation. It was a very exciting and challenging position and I enjoyed every bit of it.

I was somewhat intrigued, however, when I later received an invitation from Frank Jungers, then Assistant District Manager of Abqaiq, to meet with him at his office on November 25.

I drove to Abqaiq for the meeting. On arrival, I discovered that the Superintendent of Abqaiq's Community Services, Red Byrne, was also present for the meeting. It came as a complete surprise when Mr. Jungers asked if I would consider moving into Community Services and, more specifically, into Byrne's position of Superintendent in Abqaiq. This move would be conditional on first undergoing a two-year intensive developmental assignment both within Community Services and abroad. He took time to emphasize the importance and implications of taking on this position since I would be the first Saudi to fulfil such a role.

I can still clearly remember Mr. Jungers pointedly repeating his promise to me. He said, "If you complete the preparation in two years, the job will be yours. But you have to first go through a detailed program and then you will replace Mr. Byrne." My response was immediate and enthusiastic. "I will happily take the position if you will fulfil your promises." He agreed to do so.

Consequently, just one week later I embarked on an intensive program of developmental assignments that would expose me to the breadth of service lines covered by Aramco's Community Services department. With a thoroughness that took me from A to Z, I had to rapidly learn the ins and outs and challenges of how to keep a community functional and contented. It wasn't until much later that I realized just how extensive the developmental period would be, by which time I had neglected to consider allowing enough comparable training time for Saudis I nominated to fulfil similar positions — I just assumed they would learn on the job.

REFLECTIONS FROM FRANK JUNGERS

When I was put in charge of Abqaiq, one of our major work centers and communities, I found that the community was very upset about the caliber of their feeding facilities. I obtained the services of Ali who did an amazing job of analyzing the management problems and satisfying the needs of this sizable town. This, in turn, improved the work performance of the oil fields management whose family needs were being satisfied. He did this by

getting to know the people in the community very
quickly and then doing a superb job of keeping up
with and providing their needs.

EXPOSURE TO NEW IDEAS AT CORNELL

One part of the developmental assignment required me to spend a summer back in the United States, this time at Cornell University, New York State. Here I participated in an intensive training program offered by the Hospitality and Hotel Center. The course content was an eye-opener for me in so many ways, with a breadth of new information to absorb and assimilate. However, I appreciated the challenge and thoroughness of the approach as I was determined to run Community Services safely, efficiently and effectively and wanted to prepare accordingly.

Soon after my return, I met with a colleague who worked in Abqaiq Food Services, and I suddenly had an opportunity to put some of my newly acquired knowledge into action. He complained to me about his health, sharing that he found it difficult standing on his feet for long periods of time. Before approaching me, he had already spent several years visiting doctors without any tangible results. I suggested we go together to the Abqaiq Clinic as well as the Medical Administrator.

I had an idea about what the issue might be, and the clinic confirmed my suspicion that the employee was getting tired so quickly when standing because he had flat feet. That discovery meant he could be assigned to another position more suitable to his abilities and health, a position in which he happily remained working until he retired. I had first learned about flat feet from the program at Cornell University.

I learned a great variety of other useful things at Cornell, but not always in the classroom. One day, as I was passing the library there, I noticed an area of ground being cleared and flattened. The following day, the route to my classrooms looked markedly different when I discovered a lawn of green grass where the cleared area had previously been. I thought I must have taken a wrong turn! However, a fellow student explained that this was called 'sod grass', and that it had been previously planted and grown on an open area designed specifically for that purpose before being laid as turf in the college grounds as an instant, ready-made lawn. Apparently, I learned, the growers sold the turf by square footage, also delivering and laying it as required. A few years later, Community Services began doing the same in Riyadh, contracting a private company to complete turf installation within the Aramco facilities.

BECOMING SUPERINTENDENT

Eventually December 1967 rolled around, and I was (finally) able to assume the position of Superintendent, Abqaiq Community Services. I was immediately given full authority to manage the organization in what I saw as the most efficient and economical way possible.

My first priority at that time was to identify Saudi nationals within the organization who could fulfil the key job positions at Unit Head level. Within a year, we had developed appropriate training programs for each candidate, including some assignments in the United States which would expose them to the more advanced training on offer there through culinary institutes and technical schools as well as practical work and skills development opportunities.

By the time another year had passed, all the identified key personnel had finished their developmental programs and assumed positions of Unit Head in Food, Retail, Housing, Recreation, Gardening, Sanitation etc. It was the beginning of a new era in Abqaiq Community Services, with all key positions now filled by qualified Saudis. We had achieved my goal of complete Community Services management in Abqaiq District by a Saudi workforce, and the community welcomed the change.

Another smaller but still significant change I instigated was to introduce several popular local and national dishes into the various dining halls of the Southern Area. The rest of the company communities followed our lead in adopting these "new" local dishes onto their menus.

This menu change largely came about because during the early part of my assignment to Abqaiq, I had discovered that a large number of the working population did not eat fish regularly, especially our friends from the Najran Province. I decided to introduce some seafood dishes onto the dining hall menus to encourage them to trying something different. As a result, some did begin to enjoy eating fish. Over subsequent years, as the number of seafood eaters increased, I continued to introduce a greater variety of fish-based choices. It was eventually decided that on any day of the week a seafood dish would be available on every main menu. Residents of all nationalities indicated to me that they were appreciative of the improvements.

It took me a while to get used to all the authority I suddenly had as a Superintendent. This was illustrated one day when I received a visit from my boss, Larry Crampton. During his visit, I asked him for permission to expand the Abqaiq Commissary and build an office for the supervisor. He told me to go to the Reclamation Yard and pick up a big container (for use as the office) and then to call Merlyn Jones in Udhailiyah to request a recycled and rebuilt AC unit for it. Somewhat bemused, he went on to inform me that because the Maintenance unit was under my supervision, I was actually already authorized to request the work be undertaken and didn't need to ask for his permission.

Throughout my time in the Southern Area, I worked hard with my team on a comprehensive plan to make Abqaiq a more pleasant and desirable living environment. This was partly achieved by fostering communication with the residential community and improving their understanding of the role of Community Services as a whole. Equally as important was instilling into our busy service personnel the significance of their work within the community, and its value in making Abqaiq a nicer place to live. In this way, Abqaiq became known throughout Aramco as the "Friendly City".

I personally found the Abqaiq community friendly on many levels. Many families regularly welcomed me into their homes, including the Grimes, Pattersons, Robinsons, Boylans, and Abu Ahmed among others. Staying in Abqaiq as a bachelor was difficult: commuting to Al-Khobar in my Volkswagen was not safe, particularly when there was rough weather, such as rain or sandstorms! The generous and warm hospitality offered to me by these wonderful people made my life more comfortable and inspired me to invest further time and effort on behalf of the community overall.

We were proud of our achievements in Abqaiq and liked to acknowledge them. In June 1970, for example, we arranged for a special luncheon to be held in the Abqaiq Clubhouse to celebrate a safety record achieved by the staff of Abqaiq CS Division. Over the period October 1960 to June 1970, they managed six million man-hours worked without a disabling injury. As superintendent of the division, my role was to welcome the 160 guests and introduce the speaker, Mr. D. J. Sullivan, Senior Vice President of Operations. We gave out prizes, including portable television sets and watches on a lottery basis at the end of the event.

Under my supervision, Community Services conducted a major environmental clean-up of Abqaiq, making it aesthetically a much better and more pleasing place to live. However, developing Abqaiq as a good community went beyond just physical effort, and required further interventions, such as enhancing support for self-directed groups to make them more interesting and appealing to the residents.

Like all the other Aramco communities, Abqaiq suffered from the wider effects of an unprecedented event in 1967. Normal daily life was interrupted by the extended influence of intensified regional conflict: The Six-Day War, also known as The June War, the 1967 Arab—Israeli War or the Third Arab—Israeli War. The conflict was fought between June 5 and 10, 1967, the feuding parties being Israel and the neighboring states of Egypt, Jordan and Syria.

Increasing tensions generated in the wider region caused a good number of Aramco's dependent families to elect to leave the Kingdom. It was a rough and somewhat anxious time for the many male employees who remained behind to work and for the few families who did decide to stay, causing considerable stress within the communities. Thankfully, the situation returned to normal a short time later, as life reverted to its previous routines once again, particularly within the Abqaiq community.

During my time, Aramco's Udhailiyah (UDH) camp went through a process of mothballing and then resizing from bachelor status back to family accommodations once again. Rebuilding UDH as a community was a major task, although creating a smaller Community Services in UDH was much easier.

My position as Community Superintendent meant I often had people come to me with different personal requests. One that sticks in my mind regards a woman who asked to meet with me regarding the reconsideration of a personal effects claim she had made. I was pleased to grant her an hour-long appointment in my office, during which time we went through her claim in detail. As a result of our discussions, I told her that I would honestly only be prepared to honor three of the six items claimed.

She then tried to influence my decision by reminding me, "I am the wife of Mr. So and So."

I was already more than aware of whose wife she was and fully appreciated her husband's position within the company, but I still told her firmly, "That's all I can approve".

Next day, her husband called me and told me, "I admire you for meeting my wife and not approving everything she asked for. Furthermore," he said, "we have been married for 25 years, but I never recall being able to say no to her!"

My role as Head of Community Services in the area also meant certain types of issues and incidents were brought to my attention by Industrial Security. The majority was only minor issues and consequently, I tended to overlook most of them, especially those involving mischievous behavior by young people. I had children of similar ages, and I expected some misbehavior or pranks as part of normal growing up. There were some members of management who did not appreciate my stance on these things and wanted me to take more severe action. However, I felt that I wanted to treat people in the community more like they were family.

BILLIE TANNER NEEDED SOME
GARDENING PROBLEMS SOLVED...

*When we moved to Abqaiq, Ali invited us to his home in
the community for tea and snacks one Friday afternoon.
Ali was a most gracious host — he could converse on so
many subjects and he had a great sense of humor.*

*I had a gardener in Abqaiq who did not know how to
garden even though he was counselled repeatedly. I grew
the most beautiful periwinkles on the perimeters of my
home but the gardener would routinely cut them down
when I wasn't around to stop him. I told Ali about this.
Ali called him in and asked why he kept cutting down
Mrs. Tanner's flowers, to which he answered, "I just don't
know why I cut them down." I don't know what Ali told
him, but he never cut down my flowers again and he
remained my gardener until he retired.*

*Ali was the best Community Services manager we
ever had — our problems were always quickly resolved
in a professional manner. My memory of Ali is that he
was loyal, honest and of the highest moral integrity when
dealing with those that needed community services.*

JANE ROBINSON CLEAVER WORKED
AS A "RETURNING STUDENT"

*While I was a college 'Returning Student', I worked for
Ali and Fouad Saleh in Community Services in Abqaiq.
Ali and Mohammed Saeed Al-Ali were friends of my
parents, Opal and Curly Ball and Ali and Bobby Grimes,*

hence the familiarity of 'Ali B'. A lot of fun was ALWAYS had by ALL in that town!

Ali is and has always been kind and generous to everyone he meets — never judgmental or showing any differentiation towards who or what you were. We have had so many memorable times with him and his family over the years. I especially remember my first Saudi wedding at his home in Al-Khobar when his son was married around 1972. What a gala that was!

MOHAMMED SAEED AL-ALI FOUND A MENTOR:

In 1967, I returned from college in the United States and started work in Personnel in Abqaiq as a Personnel Advisor. Ali was in charge of Community Services there. One of my first challenges was handling a 'Termination for Cause' case involving a Saudi Arab librarian. At first, I endorsed the termination, supporting Community Services' action, but soon changed my mind and withdrew my endorsement. Instead, the employee was given a warning. Ali appreciated my position, without criticizing me. He then started teasing me about my lack of "experience."

When he first teased me with the "experience" shortcoming, I strongly opined that he should be "flexible". He said, "Yes, I can be flexible okay, but not adjustable!" This has remained our shared anecdote ever since.

1

2

1 One gentleman who had a positive influence on my career from this period onwards was Les Goss.

2 Hal Fogulquist, who also had a positive influence on my career.

3 Meeting with Saeed Muraisal in the Abqaiq Library in 1967 to discuss the out-of-Kingdom degree program that he had just returned from. I always felt it was important to help those returning from studying to apply their learning to real-life situations.

1

2

1 An Assyrian Plum
  tree on 21st Street,
  Abqaiq, planted in
  1967 when I was part of
  the community there.
  Making the communities
  more pleasant places to
  live was a goal of mine.

2 With the Grimes and
  Robinson families whose
  company I enjoyed very
  much while we were
  in Abqaiq.

3 In Abqaiq with Abdul
  Aziz Al-Hokail, 1967.

3

4

4 In the Najmah
community commissary
conferring with
Hassan Ahmed Salem,
Supervisor of Retail
Services in Ras Tanura.
This photo was featured
in an article announcing
my new position as
Superintendent of
Community Services
in Ras Tanura.
(Moody, *Arabian Sun*,
Dec 23, 1970).

5 Catching up with
Dr. Bob Oertly in
October 1996, at the
Saudi Aramco Retirees
Reunion in Florida.

5

1

2

3

1 1996 visit to William Paterson University with President Speart.

2 Visit to William Paterson University in 2018 with my wife Amira. It is important to me to keep ongoing communication with the staff there and to follow new developments.

3 Professor Parrillo and his family in younger days when I first got to know him.

4 1974 portrait for Aramco's *Arabian Sun*.

4

5

6

7

8

5 Reuniting with Larry Crampton and meeting his sister at the 1994 Saudi Aramco Retirees Reunion in Arizona.

6 With some of the first local female staff we employed in Community Services.

7 Mrs. Lynn Barrett (on right) from the Dhahran Library at a family wedding. I very much enjoy following all of my friends' family news.

8 Peggy Smith, Housing Assignment Advisor.

1

2

3

4

1. Conducting an inspection of stock in the Dhahran Commissary Chill Room in 1976 as the Commissary Department Manager.

2. Portrait for *Arabian Sun* article announcing my promotion to General Manager.

3. Getting coffee from the first vending machine in Aramco, December 1989. As General Manager, it was my privilege and prerogative to get the very first cup!

4. Recognizing Ali A. Saleh on his retirement, June 1987, a memorable occasion for me.

5 The Al-Mujamma'
Community Service
Center.

6 These iconic Aramco
buildings (the mail center,
laundry and canteen)
were amongst those
demolished to create the
parking lot for the new
centralized Al-Mujamma'
Community Service
Center.

5

6

1

1 The Cherry family visits the site of one of their earlier Dhahran homes while attending the 2019 KSA Reunion.

2 Enjoying the company of colleagues at Aramco's Heritage Gallery.

3 Fouad Saleh greets CEO John Kelberer at the opening of the refurbished Dhahran Commissary.

4 Farewell gathering with all my office and admin staff on my retirement in 1990.

5 My retirement portrait for the *Arabian Sun* newspaper with a view of the Dhahran mosque through the window.

2

4

3

5

1

2

1   A group of work colleagues and friends from across the company gathered to mark my retirement.

2   Over the years, I have been asked to make many speeches at various types of gatherings, in Arabic and English. However, I think my body language has improved since this 1978 meeting in Lebanon (top), as evidenced by my calm demeanor during my retirement speech in 1990 (bottom).

3   Officiating at ribbon-cutting ceremony at Building 198 to inaugurate a new Dhahran Personal Computer Society (DPCS) facility on September 13, 1986. I was rewarded with a certificate granting me an honorary membership for the following year, in the company of other notable "friends" of the DPCS, including Fouad Saleh, Zainal Alireza, Ali Seflan, Ahmed Al-Jassas and Richard Ksiazek (Photo: *Arabian Sun*, October 1986).

3

4

4 Presenting the trophy to community member Brenda Neal, who was the winning female runner in the Dhahran Marathon, March 2, 1984.

5 With Saleh Qabqab and Nasser Al-Ajmi.

6 With Mohammed Saeed Al-Ali and Ali Zawad. I had mentored Ali and was pleased when he became Administrator of Executive Guest Services.

5

6

1

2

1 With Abdul Majid
Al-Jamid, Manager,
Southern Area
Community Services,
and Abdul Rahim
Al-Ahmed, Aramco's
Director of Personnel.

2 With Mohammed
Salaamah and Ismail
Nawwab.

3 Jumah, Saudi Aramco
President and CEO, and
Ali Saflan, Senior Vice
President, at a biannual
gathering of Saudi
retirees.

4 All the female
Community Services
staff who gathered to
mark my retirement
including my secretary
Megan Grant.

5 My retirement citation.

3

4

1

1 At the Dhahran US Consulate Art Show in 2012 with Ambassador Smith and Mariati Messinger.

2 A 2020 meeting of the Saudi Retirees Advisory Committee of Saudi Aramco.

2

3

3 Me speaking at an event saying farewell to our guests after the 2015 KSA Reunion.

4 Enjoying some heritage at the CEO's 2016 Ramadan Ghabg'a event.

4

1

2

1   Abdul Majeed Park in
Al-Khobar, named after
a prominent Aramco
retiree.

2   I was pleased to
be present at the
opening of the
Abdul Majeed Park.

3   Our current home,
which our dear
neighbors would not
allow us to leave.

4   Our intended
retirement home.

5   A meeting of
the Dammam
Agricultural Society.

3

4

1 A meeting of
the Dammam
Agricultural Society.

2 Attendants at the 1995 bi-annual meeting for IAAPA directors and their families.

3 With Khalid Al-Mulhim as he receives an award from the President of the National Retirement Association.

2

3

1 Participating in
Al-'Ardah, the
Kingdom's traditional
sword dance.

~ 12 ~

AN INTERLUDE IN RAS TANURA

WHILE ON ASSIGNMENT in the United States, I followed my studies of food handling and related services at Cornell University with an Executive Management Program at Penn State University. Attached to the company's New York office, I gained further workplace experience in the Personnel, Purchasing and Traffic Departments. Amongst other things, this required becoming familiar with the functions of various company vendors, including the East and West Coast operations of Richmond Export.

Upon my return to the Kingdom, I was reassigned from December 1, 1970 to Ras Tanura Community Services. As Superintendent, it was a similar position to that I previously held in Abqaiq, and my responsibilities included supervising the 250 employees operating the retail outlets, recreation, food, utilities and housing services for Aramco's employees and their dependents then resident in Ras Tanura.

Arriving at the Main Gate for the first time in my new capacity as Superintendent, I was pleased to discover Yousef Al-Naimi there, waiting to welcome me. Yousef was Ali Al-Naimi's older brother and at that time, he was Aramco's Public Relations representative in Ras Tanura. We had been friends for many years, but it was still a big and pleasant surprise to be greeted by him.

I look back on my two years in Ras Tanura as a very fruitful time. Once more, I found myself directing and instituting a major training program to target, develop and upskill Saudi personnel for specific key jobs, an objective I managed to realize within my first year there. I was even able to select and prepare my replacement, a pleasing and effective piece of succession planning. Another major project was to instigate a major clean-up of the Najmah community, the first of two to be undertaken in my time within the Ras Tanura vicinity, and reaching out to include the communities of Safaniyah and Tanajib.

I recall the Najmah community being very kind to me. They opened their homes to me and were friendly and thoughtful. I have fond memories of particular families like the Gernons, Rexes, and Eals (the Area Manager and his family). The wider local management was also very supportive of my plans to improve and beautify the community.

I did experience one very serious personal incident while at Ras Tanura. One day, I went to the snack bar at the Surf House where I asked for an apple to eat. Later on that evening, I was not able to sleep because of what I thought was indigestion. The following morning, I went to the clinic. The doctor gave me a pain killer and sent me back to work. I was still suffering discomfort by the afternoon, so I went back to the clinic and asked the doctor to send me to the Dhahran Health Center for further assessment.

In Dhahran, I was seen by Dr. Robert "Bob" Oertly who administered some blood tests, sending them directly to the United States for analysis. He then treated me with antibiotics and admitted me to the Health Center. I continued to suffer during the early part of my stay at the clinic — the poor nurses had to change my bed sheets every few hours and I experienced a lot of pain. However, as the anti-biotics began to work, I started to improve.

Some of my dearest friends tried telling me that being better was actually really only a sign of impending death! They told me tall tales about people who pick up and suddenly become better but were really getting ready to say goodbye to the world! When my mother came to visit me later, she was more reassuring and genuinely pleased that I looked much improved.

While waiting for the test results, however, I was treated as a critical patient. That was later confirmed to me by a Personnel Advisor, Abdullah Al-Jama', who revealed that I had been on the DHC critical list for a time. When Dr. Oertly received the results of the tests a week later, it was clear I had experienced a bout of severe food poisoning. It was felt that the likely cause may well have been the staff member serving at the Surf House snack bar not washing his hands after using the toilet before handing me the apple.

Eventually I returned to normal, but I am in debt to Dr. Robert Oertly, who unfortunately is no longer with us, God bless his soul!

~ 13 ~

DHAHRAN: CITY OF BOSSES, 1972-1981

WHEN I BECAME Superintendent of Recreation and Residential Services in Dhahran, I quickly became known by the residents as the "go-to guy" if something needed to be done. Although I was only continuing to work the same way I had in Abqaiq and Ras Tanura, it appeared my bosses in Dhahran did not favor this approach! I had an "open door" policy, but they preferred I go through the official channels at every turn. I refused to give in and change my style to please them, continuing to apply common sense to resolve issues wherever possible while still complying with the company's policies and procedures. This inevitably caused some tension.

One area of my work in which I had already developed a long-term interest was serving on the local Recreational Library Committee wherever I worked. I believed these committees served an important educational and social role. I fondly recall the group of people I worked closely with in Dhahran, including Mrs. Jacobs and Mrs. Lynn Bennett, although there were many others as well.

A regular task for the committee members was the careful consideration of which books should be purchased for the libraries. Usually, choices were made from the wide range of books listed by major newspapers, such as the New York Times Book Review. I found it an excellent learning exercise, especially as it ensured we were providing worthwhile and welcomed additions to the existing collections in the Aramco public libraries.

I love reading. Before retirement I read more technical volumes, but now I read books with more of a social and cultural appeal, and I also enjoy regularly reading the Holy Quran. I feel strongly we should encourage our children to read according to their hobbies as well as religious texts.

LYNN BARRETT SHARES SOME EXPERIENCES AS AN ARAMCO LIBRARY COORDINATOR:

I don't remember how Ali came to know that I had a background in libraries, but it might have been from a conversation we had at a reception for the wives of new Aramco employees in September 1972. He subsequently contacted me to offer me an opportunity to contribute to the Dhahran library.

He was, and actually still is, full of energy. He was also genuinely interested in the development of Aramco's libraries and perceived what they were able to offer to the communities.

I worked for eight years as Library Coordinator for Aramco's community libraries but was based in Dhahran. During that time, Ali supported not only the improvement of the Dhahran library but also saw the

*benefits of introducing technology to improve our services
to all the community libraries.*

*When I started, magazines and newspapers from the
US were coming in by ship and, consequently, were very
out of date when they reached the library shelves. I was
told they had always been acquired in that way and
that it was good enough, but Ali got behind my request
for air shipments and won the argument. He was also
instrumental in the enlargement of the Dhahran Library
and the improvement of the libraries in the other Aramco
communities in the late seventies and early eighties.*

*I think one of the most impressive things about Ali
is his vision and his desire to learn. He has the ability
to look forward, to embrace new ideas and new ways of
doing things.*

*I believe Ali's legacy stems from his ability to always
look to the future. He brought Community Services, and
the libraries in particular, up to date and appreciated the
wants and needs of new employees and their families,
which were different from the families that came in
earlier days. He helped to make working for Aramco
exciting.*

HONING MY DIPLOMACY!

Hard work paid off for me and on April 1, 1974 when I was appointed
to the newly created post of Assistant Manager of Community
Services Operations. In the organizational structure, I now found
myself responsible for more than 1000 staff employed in food and
retail outlets, recreational facilities and residential services. The

list of divisions that now reported directly to me (at least for a few months!) included: Food and Retail Services, Recreation and Residential Services in Dhahran, and Community Services in Abqaiq, Ras Tanura and the Northern Area (this included Turaif, Badanah, Rafha, Qaisumah and Safaniyah). A re-organization of Community Services was then conducted by the McKenzie Group, converting the organization into six departments. In the new structure, I was appointed Manager of the Food Distribution Department.

Residential housing was one of the major undertakings of Community Services, with housing allocations made to company employees based on grade code and length of service. My previous community experience had already made me much more knowledgeable about community affairs and a much wiser man in administering them, so I was well-prepared to tackle the great variety of issues and concerns among the community' residents. It was rather a thankless task as it was nearly impossible to please everyone, especially when dealing with the differing expectations of the various nationalities and cultures. My philosophy was to deal with the housewives, who were generally the responsible and accountable person in every household, releasing the husbands to concentrate on doing their daily tasks without having to worry about if and when the plumber or carpenter would arrive! It seemed some members of management even became jealous of me because I spent my time dealing with so many ladies! However, dealing with the ladies was still difficult and required much diplomacy and careful negotiation. Some were even "hot" to deal with!

I recall there were some wives who put a lot of pressure on their husbands to get a promotion just so they could improve their housing entitlement choices. Therefore, it was important for me to have good staff who could handle the pressure well. I particularly remember a lady named Mary Jane Hanna who was highly effective in her role as Housing Assignments Administrator, becoming prominent and well-known amongst Dhahran residents.

Most people appreciated any effort made on their behalf. Nevertheless, the range and variety of issues and challenges we had to tackle meant we had to be flexible in our approaches whilst being seen to treat everyone fairly. There were many instances when someone would complain they weren't getting the same treatment as one of their neighbors had previously received. Overall though, beginning from my times in Abqaiq and Ras Tanura, I found the community residents to be kind, helpful and understanding and I remain indebted to so many for making my work so joyful and worthwhile.

PEGGY J. SMITH RECALLS THE CHALLENGES OF WORKING IN THE HOUSING DEPARTMENT

My first job working for Aramco was in Personnel, which gave me the opportunity to meet people and learn more about what was going on in the company. While I was working there, I heard the position of "Housing Assignments Advisor" was open.

When I applied, it was Ali Baluchi who interviewed me. I already knew of Ali through casual situations, as our Dhahran Camp wasn't very large and even going to the Commissary for food one would soon recognize others. Anyways, he interviewed me and was very pleasant but emphasized the challenge of being careful to ensure employees' points were correctly evaluated in order for them to be eligible for certain types of houses.

The housing allocation system was based on points, some based on length of service with company, some based on position, etc., so a few points could make a difference as to whether an employee qualified for certain houses. For all the expatriates, being so far from home meant their houses were of utmost importance, and Ali knew well that to keep the "peace" in our camp was extremely important. If a family (particularly the lady) wasn't happy, that could interfere with a husband and his job!

In our interview, Ali was firm, to the point and thorough. He even made me wonder if I had the confidence in myself to do the job! That was really important as, after I was hired for the position of "Housing Advisor," I found myself responsible for renting (keeping occupied) and maintaining all housing records for approximately 1,100 family houses in the Dhahran Camp. Ali was well aware of the fact that family housing retained employees on the payroll by keeping them happy, otherwise Aramco would lose them and their talent. It was sometimes difficult, particularly for the wife, to accept the fact that her husband didn't quite have enough points for a larger house or a house in a different part of the camp.

What most impressed me about Ali was the way he greeted everyone in a friendly manner and made all of us feel so welcome in his country. That is a major reason as to why he was so effective at managing housing — I don't think he ever "met a stranger," as the saying goes.

CITY OF BOSSES

Dhahran was known as the "City of Bosses," and that was certainly my experience! Although my managers were all highly educated people and well-qualified for their original positions, they usually moved into Community Services from other areas of company operations. This meant many were not always wise or sensitive to the particular challenges and subtleties of providing services to residents in the company communities. Most often, the company "parked" them in these positions so they could extend for a couple of years in order to reach retirement and gain some additional benefits. Because of the nature of their management responsibilities, I was told to help them, and I was generally happy to do so. Some were even sympathetic to my position and disappointed that I was not actually allowed to run the show.

When the stress finally got under my skin, I remember Frank Jungers came to visit me in the hospital. I confessed to Frank how frustrating I had found things, having to deal with one particular guy who understood so little about community services and who was consequently doing such a poor job of decision making, and yet still I was expected to refer to him as my boss! Jungers encouraged me not to take it so hard. He said, "Ali, don't let it upset you; the future is coming and one day you will be in charge."

Even in those days, Aramco was still reticent to put Saudis in the key jobs, afraid that if they put them in strategic positions, they would not be able to later remove or reassign them. The company decision-makers tended to be cautious, wanting to be sure in advance that any particular Saudi would make a responsible and successful manager or superintendent, and not wanting to gamble away any opportunities. These were painful years for some of my Saudi colleagues!

Because of this disparity, a group of about 10 senior Saudis (including myself) requested a meeting with Sheikh Ahmed Zaki Yamani, the Oil Minister, at House 17 in Dhahran. We spent an hour or so discussing with him our feelings about the slowness of Saudi advancements and promotions to higher positions within the company. We shared our complaints about how much of our time seemed to be wasted on "development assignments" while we waited for positions to be vacated by retiring expats.

In answer to his assertion that we should not expect promotions just because we were Saudis, we stressed that our intent was not promotion for the sake of it, but just fairer opportunities for those who were properly qualified and had already demonstrated competence. We all felt ready and capable of performing well in key positions.

Sheikh Yamani took on board our complaints, and it wasn't too long before things started to change.

I always found Sheikh Yamani to be a kind and humble person. The cooks and waiters at House 17 always respected and thought highly of him as he treated them so politely. In fact, on several occasions he even ate breakfast with them during his stays! I have also heard that around the time of the official royal inauguration of the Juaimah gas project in Ras Tanura, Sheikh Yamani cooked for King Khalid at House 17, preparing the special meal known as marqooq — it was known to be the king's personal favorite.

Throughout this time, I also continued to visit and stay in the outlying areas whenever there were functions that needed my presence. The Trans-Arabian Pipeline, or Tapline, ran from Saudi Arabia to the Mediterranean, and during the 1970s, all housing, community and recreational services in the maintenance communities along its route reported to the central office in Dhahran. It was part of my job to arrange for their daily needs to be appropriately met and to ensure the four communities were well-managed. Logistically, everything they needed was shifted in by either air or land transportation for the duration of the project. These communities were primarily occupied by native Saudis and were mostly well run and economically stable.

I visited the four stations once every three weeks and spent a couple of nights in each area. Being physically present within these towns helped me ensure they were being well looked after in order to maintain a high morale amongst the residents, including the expats. I found the expat workers and their families particularly appreciative and generous to their visitors and guests. My objective was always to ensure that the managers of the various gas and oil projects were well-served by employees and that their families who were both happy and comfortable.

There are many interesting stories about the Tapline communities and the interactions between the local people and the Americans — many fond relationships were built. I have in my collection of papers a Saudi newspaper article about the history of Tapline where Sadeeq Ahmed, a Pakistani, described the characteristics of the locals as generous, truthful and hospitable. Ahmed stressed that the legacy of the Americans was hard work and access to education, allowing many of the local people to progress onwards into different professions.

FRED BLANCHARD DESCRIBES BEING A COLLEAGUE BEFORE BECOMING A FRIEND:

My initial contact with Ali was when he became Manager of Community Services back in the mid-1970s. Not in his capacity as manager of the Dhahran community but as the head of the organization that managed the Camps Program. I initiated the Camps Program that was an

effort to house over 30,000 contractor personnel in camps
scattered from Udhailiyah to Tanajib as part of the Master
Gas Program, the largest privately financed megaproject
ever (the program ran over one billion dollars in the 1970s
and early 1980s). That I never heard of any problems
about this program that went on for nearly 10 years attests
to Ali's ability to manage effectively.

COMMISSARY MATTERS

After attending a Middle Management training program at Harvard, I took up the position as Manager of the Food Distribution Department. Always keen to see where improvements could be made, I started by commissioning the department to conduct a survey of the commissaries in Abqaiq, Dhahran, Al-Munirah and Ras Tanura. We had about 1,500 responses to the survey and, as a result, we were able to consider introducing new food items that would suit different groups within the Aramco communities. My view was that the stores had to become more international and properly reflect the changing diversity and demographics of the communities.

We ordered the first few items on a specialty basis in order to test consumer responses. These items included sugar-free gum, water chestnuts, soybeans, marshmallows, papayas, pizza mix, avocados and assorted frozen dips, diet drinks and lighter fluid. We also sent test orders for canned 7-Up, Fritos and Alpen breakfast cereal, as well as cleaning products such as Comet, Lysol, Woolite, Mr. Soft fabric softener and Zud stainless steel sink cleaner.

It was always a tricky task to decide which brands we should order for certain other products like hair sprays, hair conditioners, cosmetics and health foods, and we encouraged the consumers to tell us their preferences through suggestion boxes placed in the various commissaries or by directly mailing the Community Services Planning and Programs Department. We also assigned a number of highly competent ladies in each commissary to stay in touch with the consumers to gauge their ongoing responses to the changes.

Some items were requested so often that we put them directly on Aramco's regular order list. These included products like Velveeta cheese, sour cream mix, refried beans, honey granola, macaroni and cheese, frozen onion rings, furniture wax, Oreo cookies, soft drinks, beef burgers, tortillas and jalapenos. Looking back, these foods reflect what was popular at the time, and there are some major differences today.

Another challenge was meeting the demand for more choice of fresh fruit and vegetables, so orders were placed for air shipments of high-quality produce from Lebanon and Iran to supplement the local and Dutch-sourced produce. We paid special attention to Abqaiq and Ras Tanura where we increased produce shipments to three times each week, and also ensured that unannounced shipments of fruit and vegetables from Lebanon or other sources would be delivered to outlying communities on the day of arrival wherever possible.

Further difficulties were encountered in sourcing items such as fresh fish and meat, which were only available in limited quantities and at high prices. Expanding our range of frozen items was limited by the warehouse storage space available at the time, but we did go on to improve our freezer storage capacity. We also increased the number of check-out counters in the Dhahran commissary from seven to 10 to alleviate long queues at certain busy times.

While I was the manager of the Food Distribution Department, we were able to attract one of the first professional Saudi women to the workforce, Nahid Al-Gossaibi, a graduated from the American

University of Beirut, who was hired in Food Quality Control. She did a commendable job and opened the door for us to hire some other young Saudi women. I am proud to say that I was among only a few Saudi managers who generated wider support for hiring qualified young Saudi women after they had completed their college educations.

In my capacity as departmental manager, I undertook an assignment in the United States with grocery store chain the Great Atlantic & Pacific Tea Company (or A&P). This subsequently prepared me for completing a bachelor's degree in Business Administration, followed closely by a master's in Social Science at William Paterson University. Further to this, my position changed in 1980 to Manager of the combined Food Processing and Distribution Department.

I owe this opportunity to one particular American colleague who supported my case for further education and training. His name was Mr. Les Goss, an excellent engineer and a kind and sincere man with a good judgement of others. He was a great example to me, the sort of character who would tell you straight if you were being arrogant or difficult, but if you deserved it, would praise you for doing well. It was he and company Vice President Bob Ryrholm who agreed to give me the assignment to New Jersey with A&P. It meant I would also get the opportunity to complete my studies at night school.

While I was in America, A&P came to Dhahran and managed my job in Community Services in my stead, both heading up the commissary and implementing planned improvements. Meanwhile, during the day I worked for them in management in New Jersey and after I finished up, I went to night school at William Paterson University. After finishing work at 4:00 p.m., I would drive to my home (about half an hour away from the office) and attend class from 6:00 to 10:00 p.m., five days a week. Saturday and Sunday were days off work but on Saturdays I took a class from 10:00 a.m. to 12:00 and then spent another couple of hours in the library. On Sundays, I would also go to the library and mostly stayed until they closed at 8:00 p.m. I remember one day they locked the library up while I was still inside! Luckily they had those emergency doors that can only be opened from the inside, so I still managed to get out.

On completion of my master's degree, A&P specially commended me for my achievement − they had never before engaged a student who was able to complete the two-year college master's degree program in the space of one year, as I had done.

During the time I was studying at the university, my late wife Sharifa came for a visit to New Jersey with a few of my children; they were all very excited about the prospect of spending the summer with me. However, they suffered one week of my routine, and then in the second week, she told me that they hadn't come all that way just to eat and sleep while I worked. She wanted me to take them out and about to New York, Washington, Disneyworld and other tourist destinations.

I told her she was talking to the wrong guy: I wasn't there for a holiday and my object was to get my degree, to work, learn more, gain further experience in management styles and how to manage the commissary and food distribution business, and then to go to school at night to finish up my degree. Disappointed, they went home to Saudi Arabia.

Over the ensuing years, I have continued my involvement with the William Paterson University Foundation by providing donations and establishing a scholarship fund under my name. I have continued to visit the university often as part of my schedule when I am travelling in the United States, and always enjoy catching up with my old friends there, hearing about ongoing and future developments. My education had a very significant impact on my life and I am pleased to now be able to help others.

EXTRACT FROM A LETTER RECEIVED FROM A LIBERAL ARTS MAJOR AT WILLIAM PATERSON UNIVERSITY

By awarding me the Ali M. Baluchi Scholarship, you have eased my financial burdens of worrying how I will be able to afford to pay for the semester AND a new computer. I now feel confident that I will succeed in achieving my dreams in the creative world and will be able to fully focus and grasp the concepts I learn in my classes, and apply them towards my future.

Your generosity has inspired me to help others, just as you have helped me. I hope to be able to give a young, curious, artistic student the encouragement and faith that you have just given me.

LENKA KOSTIKOVA

PROF. VINCENT N. PARRILLO COMMENTS ON SURMOUNTING CULTURAL DIFFERENCES

Ali was a student in one of my classes at William Paterson University about 40 or so years ago. What impressed me about Ali first was his intelligence on fine display in the classroom. Next came his friendliness, then kindness and generosity. He hosted a dinner for his classmates, became a donor to the university. On a subsequent visit when he came to my house, he brought large, stuffed Sesame Street figures

*for my daughters. Other times he would invite various friends,
including myself, to a restaurant for dinner for all of us to
intermingle and especially (for me) to enjoy his company.*

*My grown daughters still remember Ali from that one
visit when he brought those super-large stuffed toys to them!*

*I think his humanity is what registered the most, not
only with me but with others. He is such a kind and good
man that he easily bridged the cultural gulf between us.
When he asked about our families or personal well-being,
you had the sense that he really cared and was not just
being socially proper. We had a high comfort level in all
conversations with each other. The differences in nationality,
culture, and religion were never once any concern in the real
friendship we enjoy with this wonderful man.*

*As long as our memories remain, his legacy will be our
recall of a barrier-free friendship and outreach to others, a
relationship that easily surmounted differences so that we
thoroughly enjoyed each other's company.*

DR. AHMED AL-SHUWAIKHAT RECALLS
A MENTORING EXPERIENCE

*In 1977, I graduated with a BA in English and Education
from Riyadh University. Since 1974, as the son of an
Aramco "old timer," it had become a pleasant routine for
me to join Aramco each year as a summer student, applying
to a different department every session. I was lucky to meet
Ali that summer of 1977 and work under his supervision
in Community Services and Recreation. I stepped into his
office in the iconic administration building in Dhahran and*

*he received me with a warm greeting. "Welcome to Aramco,
and we wish you a productive and educational experience,"
he said. "What are you expecting from your work with us?"*

*I answered eagerly, expressing my desire to work in
the entertainment complex where the cinema, library,
swimming pool and bowling room were, and still are.*

*"Alright, you got it," Ali told me, "you will work in
Recreation as you wish, and we expect you to learn and
contribute." He instructed gently, in a form of a cordial
suggestion.*

*When I expressed my gratitude, Ali added, "In two
weeks or so, the American country singer Kenny Rogers
and his band are performing in Dhahran, and you might
like to be a member of Aramco's accompanying team and
participate in helping the guests get around." I responded
enthusiastically.*

*It had been a rich first meeting during which Ali
demonstrated in minutes some of his leading faculties
in administration, educational guidance and genuine
fruitful initiatives. He had been generous, perceptive, and
considerate as ever, introducing me to a work environment
that I loved to be part of. I still remember the experiences
in detail.*

*At the end of the summer, I stepped back into Ali's
office to thank him, and he asked me about my career
plans. When I explained I was headed for the University
of San Francisco, he reached for his black telephone book,
saying, "Excellent. The Bay Area is fantastic. We have a
good friend in San Francisco named Paul who is one of
our former Aramco employees, and you both might want to*

meet him. I will call him today and tell him you will be in
San Francisco next week. You can then call him to set up
the meeting, okay?"

I could sense Ali's intent to alleviate my homesickness,
especially given that I had travelled so little abroad and was
barely 22 years old. Over a cup of tea, Ali was able to bring
people from different cultures together. No doubt, he also
wanted me to step into an environment with some kind of
support from an old friend of his.

I called Paul on my arrival and we had a nice dinner
with an inspiring chat. Paul showed me photos of places
and people in many social occasions inside and outside
Aramco. It was a journey through my culture in Paul's eyes,
through the towns and villages of Qatif, Saihat, Dammam
and Al-Khobar. I thought Paul had recorded very important
segments of the history and life in the Eastern Province of
Saudi Arabia.

I owe much to Ali who participated in shaping my views
of Saudi Aramco as a cultural and human platform, a vivid
hope where there are always the bonds of friendship among
peoples from different nations and cultures. There is much
more to Saudi Aramco than mere oil, gas and fueling the
world's hunger for energy.

A FEW MORE MEMORIES

I remember an occasion when Larry Crampton, then Dhahran's
Assistant District Manager, invited me to a meeting in his office to
investigate a teenager accused of stealing the Volkswagen emblems
from several cars in camp. Crampton started by asking the young

man's mother if she thought her son was guilty, but she turned instead to her son and asked him to respond personally. The young man admitted freely that collecting the emblems and badges was a hobby of his. Crampton explained to his mother that her son would be banned from Saudi Arabia for two years. The mother replied that in that case, she would have to go out with him, a decision that was her personal choice. I later learned that, as a result, the father threatened to quit his job and that his boss had told him it was okay.

Another memory I have involving Larry Crampton was when he called and asked me to meet him one day at Safaniyah. I didn't check the flight schedule from Dhahran, and apparently neither did he. I drove my Volkswagen to Safaniyah, but my arrival created something of a surprise for its Superintendent of Community Services, even after I explained that I was there for a meeting at Mr. Crampton's request. Shortly thereafter, Larry called, and apologized profusely for having not come because there were no scheduled flights that day. Years later, I met Larry at one of the United Stations reunions where he introduced me to his sister, and I told her the story about Safaniyah. He was a physically fit man and always pleasant to work with.

During my time in Community Services, I thoroughly enjoyed the routine of high school and college students returning from their schools elsewhere in the world to spend the summers or New Year holidays with their parents. The Recreation leadership played a constructive role in helping develop meaningful activities to make students' time here as enjoyable and constructive as possible. Industrial Security, however, claimed it was more of a nightmare for them in the late evenings, tracking the high-spirited behavior of the kids. I recall Saeed Somali, a night foreman in Dhahran. He was a nice guy who had sympathy for the kids' behavior and was

well-loved by both the returning students and community. Dear
Saeed passed away in 2016 and is survived by his lovely family who
live in my neighborhood, Al-Khobar West.

QUENT (JACK) DAVIES RECOUNTS POSITIVE
EXPERIENCES OF WORKING TOGETHER:

*We had a big fire in Abqaiq in the mid-1970s and I went
down to help out. I was in Dhahran at the time and was
assigned to help Larry Tanner rebuild the facilities after
the fire. This was a politically sensitive subject because the
Japanese stock market went into crisis because we were
their primary oil provider. World investors, politicians
etc. thought there was no longer any Abqaiq, so no oil
for Japan, therefore a big economic risk. They flew in
journalists from Europe and busloads came down from the
Dhahran airport.*

*Our job was to rebuild the 100 acres of fire damaged
facilities where they take the sulfur out of the gas (the
transition point between field and well and Abqaiq).
I was working 12-hour days, alongside 1000s of
people, including the entire workforces of other support
companies.*

*Ali at the time was working in Community Services.
Do you know those stainless-steel containers you serve
coffee in? Well, they had a few of those and used to put
coffee around dining hall and common areas. I went to
him and told him that we have a lot of people out working
who need water, orange juice, and coffee. To save time,
we don't want anyone, like welders for instance, to leave*

and go for coffee; we need to have a place for them to
replenish themselves on site. Ali said, "Yep, what do you
need?" I said, "I'd like to gather up all of those stainless-
steel containers and fill them with ice and orange juice —
whatever you've got to drink — and bring them to the
field." He responded, "Rather than have everyone bring a
chitty (under normal operations, if you had a chitty, we
gave you a jug of ice), I will open a service order and you
just come and get it." That was a huge change and showed
that he was a team player. He would solve your problem
in his own unique way. I'm sure he was criticized for that
because he was out of the ordinary, but I thought that his
unorthodox style will help him move up.

Over the years, I had a lot of interaction with Ali.
In Yanbu, we had control of the manifest for the airplane
and enjoyed the thrill of getting people on and off the
plane. Ali would sometimes need a favor, so we would help.
We had a problem where the ladies would come over for a
medical appointment or job had no place to wait. Often,
they had kids with them and had to wait in the dining hall
or Steineke for the bus to take them to the plane. Ali came
up with the idea — let's give you a house (so much more
than what we expected) right here in front of the dining
hall with a refrigerator and a freezer. He's someone who
always did more than expected in everything he did.

He's also very broadminded. He knew that some things
he engaged in may have their sensitivities, but he was
unafraid to pursue them. Afterall, he was long exposed to
expats. When you're out there on Operations you can feel
that nobody's willing to help you and, in the end, you have

to fight for everything. For instance, Ali worked for Les Goss, who greatly appreciated him. I worked directly for him when Manager of Operations, but he was taken out of Operations and put in Community Services. Les was a dynamic worker (he always had four phones on the desk) and Ali was part and parcel to that, running around constantly. He had a real job with real impact. Les would say "see Ali" if you ever needed anything. I don't know what motivated him to be as good as he was.

~ 14 ~

LESSONS FROM LEADERSHIP, 1981-1990

MY MANAGEMENT TRAINING continued into the 1980s. I completed the Rutgers Advanced Management Program at Rutgers, The State University of New Jersey in 1980, followed by an Advanced Management Seminar for Senior Executives organized by Harvard University in 1981. These courses helped prepare me for my promotion to the position of General Manager of Community Services. This was the same position I eventually retired from on April 1, 1990.

In my first year as General Manager, I was humbled to also be awarded a citation in the 1981 Marquis "Who's Who in the World" biographical reference volume, an accomplishment based on career achievements and social contributions deemed inspirational others. I was listed amongst the world's "Five Hundred Leaders of Influence."

As the 1980s progressed and significant developments continued within Aramco, it became apparent that a number of major community projects were necessary. These projects included the rebuilding and modernization of our existing commissaries and dining halls and the provision of other supporting facilities such as the Ad Diwan meeting room complex and a centralized, more user-friendly centralized hub for Community Services. An earlier program had already witnessed many of the older housing stock being demolished, rebuilt and upgraded. Such developments always fostered much appreciation and satisfaction within the residential communities as they generally much improved the living and working environment for everyone. The subsequent challenges for us, however, included the employment of a fresh and more highly skilled workforce to ensure the new facilities were properly managed and maintained.

The change to Saudi ownership of Aramco in 1980 gave impetus to discovering new ways to do business. A new vision, with a more local orientation, offered some radical opportunities for change. The prevalent management mindset actively encouraged that change to be rapid. One important goal that impacted everyone was the requirement to operate and manage all the various departments more uniformly, taking into account any local needs and adaptations to ensure a smooth modus operandi.

Within Community Services, I prioritized an "open door" policy to encourage the workforce to bring forward any grievances. However, it is well-known that in 10 years, I did not personally receive or hear a grievance from any of my employees. It was not an easy thing to achieve, but I considered it a positive challenge. "A happy work environment" became the motto of our daily business. Thanks to God, it worked well.

To help achieve this I continued to encourage ongoing education and training within the workplace as I believed it improved the overall performance and morale of the employees. I pushed my team leads to create an environment where employees were always welcome to enquire about anything they didn't know or understand, thus allowing growth and development. Throughout my own life, I have learned the value of seeking self-improvement in all we do.

One of many significant projects I saw to completion in this period was the development of the Al-Mujamma' building in Dhahran, purposed to become the hub for Community Services — a function it still effectively performs to this day. Built on the site of the old commissary and icehouse, it was opened towards the end of 1985. It was an elegant yet functional building, allowing for the centralization of all services under one roof, thereby creating convenience for employees and community residents alike. It also enabled us to consolidate the operation of departmental functions more efficiently and with a better quality of service delivery.

I recall meeting with Ismail Nawwab, General Manager of Public Affairs, to discuss and finally determine the proposed name of the service center. "Al-Mujamma" was agreed upon as the most appropriate choice. I also obtained his consent for using the name "Ad Diwan" for the new community all-purpose meeting room in the King's Road complex. This facility was another major project of the time, designed for flexible use with the inclusion of a large function room and smaller meeting rooms to meet the various needs of both the company and the growing community.

The construction of the Al-Mujamma' building took 18 months to complete, and in the process, many familiar and iconic community landmarks were removed. The old Housing Office, Building 1249 (which housed the Community Information Center and Food Services), the laundry, travel office, barber shop and mail center all disappeared in the name of progress, vanishing forever under the new car parking lot adjacent to the service center. The services themselves gained a more contemporary re-incarnation within the spacious new facility.

We endeavored to make a seamless transition of services both into and within the new facility. I recall that employees retained their previous mailbox numbers but were sent letters advising them of the combination for accessing their new box. At that time, we also installed a ticket window for the Aramco Employees' Association so tickets for their events could be purchased at regular times throughout the week. The establishment of the new "Welcoming Center," where information about the company and community was readily accessible, was received enthusiastically by both the residents and others. I am pleased that the Community Information Center is still an integral part of the service center today.

I presided over a host of changes during my decade as General Manager, some of which we probably take for granted now. One small example was the coming of vending machines into service within Aramco on Dec 2, 1989. As General Manager, I was privileged to have the honor of pressing the button and receiving the first cup of coffee!

The machines were initially trialed in four of the company's core area locations, within the Tower, EXPEC and the South Admin buildings. Representatives from the Dammam-based vending company were on hand for the first week to help with any technical difficulties while consumers got used to the new machines. It was always important for me to get customer feedback on any new initiatives, so suggestion boxes were placed at each of the machines to receive ideas, compliments or complaints.

One bittersweet task associated with my position was that of hosting service award events and luncheons for staff of Community Services who reached significant career milestones or retirement. It meant a lot to me to be able to personally recognize the achievements of so many employees. One such was Ali A. Saleh of Abqaiq, who retired in 1987. Over the course of his 35-long year career, he had risen from the position of a clerk in the Ras Tanura laundry to Manager of Southern Area Community Services. I recall he particularly enjoyed his last position as manager, and especially appreciated working with people of all nationalities, many of whom he deemed as "precious friends who shall remain friends forever". This was a sentiment I strongly shared with him.

MY SECRETARY, MEGAN GRANT

While working as secretary to Larry French, the manager of Community Services in Ras Tanura, I often had dealings with Ali in his role as the General Manager of the whole Community Services organization of Aramco. Ali's organizational skills, professionalism and kindness created an office environment that was a good and enjoyable place to work.

As a supervisor, he was truly an inspiration to his staff. His strong leadership skills, along with the support and dedication he showed to his team, earned him much deserved respect and admiration, which continued long after he retired. I feel lucky to have been a member of his staff across those years.

I moved to Dhahran in 1988 and was very lucky to be offered the position of Ali's secretary, which I held until he retired. We discovered that we share the same birthday!

Ali contributed so much to the company and to the community in general across all his long years with Aramco. He is a good and kind man who is remembered with affection by everyone who knew him.

Another pleasant aspect of my work was oversight of the various self-directed groups within the Dhahran community. I always endeavored to ensure their smooth operation with the provision of suitable facilities to meet their ongoing needs. Since the earliest days of Community Services, the company maxim had been "A satisfied man is an asset to Aramco," so the comfort and recreational enjoyment of the employees was always taken as seriously as was possible.

I was often invited to special events hosted by these self-directed groups to present trophies and awards or to officially open new facilities. As General Manager, I devoted a great deal of time to developing a sense of community with the residents, listening to their opinions and suggestions and then doing whatever was required to maintain a sense of communication both upwards and downwards.

I am gratified to see that since I retired from Saudi Aramco, additional facilities have continued to be added within the various communities. The motto of Community Services these days seems to be "we listen and care," with many new options involving the use of outside contractors to serve the overall community — no mean task considering the residents now hail from around one hundred different ethnicities and nations. This plethora of sports and recreational facilities abounds in response to an overall growing awareness of the importance of nurturing healthy lifestyles in the Kingdom and in response to the increase in expatriate residents' expectations, in line with what's on offer in their home communities elsewhere in the world. My wife Amira and I like to take our exercise by walking circuits in the air-conditioned comfort of the Dhahran Mall.

Looking back over my Aramco career, there are a number of achievements I have found particularly satisfying, the most important one probably being able to assist in the professional development of so many Saudi nationals, especially through my contribution to the overall Saudization of Community Services. By the time of my retirement, all positions of unit, division and departmental heads were filled by Saudis, with several of these moving forward to other assignments elsewhere in the organization where they were to hold very senior positions, including that of Vice President.

I was able to encourage a good number of Saudis to further their educations by studying for degrees in areas such as business, the social sciences and the culinary arts. Among others, names that spring to mind include Ahmed Hussein Saleh (manager of the construction camps); Abdullah Mattar (Food Services), Abdul Majid Al-Jamid (Abqaiq Community Services) and Saeed Al-Ghamdi (Manager of Central Community Services).

I also consider it a significant achievement that I was able to persuade management to remove the college degree and technical diploma requirements from many positions where relevant and constructive experience and demonstrated competency could be considered sufficient. This allowed the advancement of even more Saudis.

In 1975, Aramco found itself competing with SABIC, SCCECO and some other major employers in the Kingdom, to attract and retain Saudi staff. Looking for a solution to give Aramco an edge, we convinced management of the benefits of allowing young Saudis with college degrees to live in the residential camps, rather than making them wait until they achieved the higher grades code of 14+. This proved to be an attractive proposition for many young Saudis considering joining the company at that time.

MOHAMMED SAEED AL-ALI COMMENTS
ON SUPPORT FOR LOCALS

Ali is a very well-known and much-loved figure in a number of towns, including Qatif and Al-Hasa. His help was frequently sought by an employee, or the son of one, for work with Aramco or for a transfer to another job, especially in his last position as General Manager of Community Services. Many of his contemporaries did not have the opportunity to achieve advanced school qualifications, so he gave them access to heavy doses of on-the-job training to help qualify them for promotions.

But Ali did not make it easy for people. I recall one instance when an employee demanded promotion to Grade Code 11 and Ali told him that if he could convince the supervisor of Personnel, only then would he seriously consider promoting him, and he did!

JOAN CHERRY REMEMBERS SHARING
A MEMORABLE DESSERT

In October or November 1983, we lived at a place called North Camp, a triple wide trailer camp community somewhere near Dhahran. I was a young bride back then, still "green" shall we say with regard to my cooking and baking skills. At the time, we had just gotten to know Ali.

One day, we invited Ali over for lunch. I do not remember what was on the menu for that day, but

*the dessert I made is a story in and of itself. It was
a chocolate potato pound cake. I was preparing
my cake in the kitchen, assembling the ingredients
and had started mixing the batter when I realized
that I needed another egg or another cup of sugar
(I'm not sure which). When I went next door to
ask a neighbor, she asked me to stay for coffee, and
I did. Several hours later, I went back to my batter
which was already mixed but missing the last few
ingredients. The batter was a strange consistency,
but I baked the cake anyway.*

*Lunch went well, but my cake was NOT very
good, and I was embarrassed and hoped no one would
notice. Ali performed his due diligence and commented
on how good lunch was. I prayed there was not going
to be another critique of the dessert portion of lunch,
but no, that prayer was never answered.*

*In my recollection, he stated again that lunch was
good, but the cake, he said while shaking his head
disapprovingly, was "dry, dry, dry!"*

*He certainly wasn't wrong, and I did feel rather
bad for quite a long time. I'm long since over the
shame of it, and the story has since become infamous
and a favorite "inside joke" with our family. If one
of my meals has been overcooked, or if we go out to
a restaurant and something is burned, or just not
good, one of us will shake our heads disapprovingly
and utter "dry, dry, dry!" and break out in a laugh!
We love you, Ali!!!!! (Incidentally, the chocolate pound
cake went on to become my signature cake!).*

ROBERT ERIKSON RECALLS WORKING
IN COMMUNITY SERVICES:

I arrived in Dhahran in February of 1977, hired as part of a newly organized Community Services facilities planning group. Ali was Manager of Commissary Services, which was one of the Departments in the Community Services Administrative Area and the acting Head of Community Services at the time was Ali Al-Naimi.

On first meeting, Ali had a certain stature, a way of carrying himself that indicated he was a man to take seriously and listen to when he spoke. There was a business-like toughness to him and a lead-by-example manner for all the new arrivals to see and understand. He seemed to be someone who demanded and expected excellence from those who worked for him.

Eight or nine years later, after I had handed over two of my positions to Saudis, I thought I might find myself without a job. By this time, Ali was General Manager of Community Services. I went to talk with him about my situation and he assured me that he would help and that I would be placed in a new position, which I was. I was grateful to Ali then and still to this day.

A TALE OF FOUAD MOHAMMED SALEH

I did not always get what I wanted, as the following tale illustrates.

I remember one particular incident involving myself and Dr. Taylor, Medical Director of the Dhahran Health Organization. We ended up having something of a protracted tug-of-war over the employment status of one of his Health Prevention Advisors, Fouad Mohammed Saleh.

I knew Fouad would be an asset to Community Services with the potential to have a significant impact on our behalf. I tried hard to entice him to join us. Initially, I approached Dr. Taylor about a transfer, but he responded negatively, citing that the Health Organization had invested a lot of money and time in developing Fouad's skills already.

A few weeks passed and I received a request from Fritz Taylor, Vice President of Industrial Relations, to attend a meeting in his office. On arrival, I found Dr. Taylor also present. It transpired that Dr. Taylor had made a complaint to Fritz regarding my desire to acquire Fouad's talents for Community Services. I admitted I was keen to poach Fouad as I had a position suitable for him that he could fill very effectively following a short developmental assignment. After much discussion, Fritz told Dr. Taylor that unless he promoted Fouad very soon, he would be transferred to Community Services. Fouad was eventually promoted to the position of Supervisor of Health Prevention.

Over the years, Fouad never forgot my eagerness for him to be part of Community Services. Another opportunity to transfer came later, and Fouad told management how I had previously so enthusiastically endorsed his potential. I was so pleased when management accepted his arguments and allowed him to transfer across. Fouad rose to become Vice President of Community, Building and Office Services before he retired from Saudi Aramco.

In my personal opinion, Fouad did a great job during his tenure in Community Services, particularly by modernizing and developing better facilities for company employees. He was also responsible for the development of the Community Heritage Gallery, the small museum and archive of Aramco and its communities, sited within the Main Camp on the intersection of 12th and Ibis streets.

CONTINUOUS IMPROVEMENT

Throughout my management tenure, my own teams worked hard at continuously improving the various facilities and services available to the employees and their families. We were under pressure to stay in line with the demands of changing global standards and the consequent rising community expectations. To do this, we hired some major international retailing companies to implement upgrades or manage our facilities, including Marriott and the Atlantic and Pacific Tea Company. Because they were experts in their fields, management listened and was sympathetic to the changes they suggested.

Of course, the availability of the necessary funding was also always a key issue in seeing desired changes come into effect. However, collaboration with international companies also opened up opportunities to send out some of our key personnel for training and development overseas. The companies themselves generally brought in good supervisors to oversee their projects, but we ensured it was Saudis who did the basic work.

I believe my personal and professional values were greatly enriched by working and living in proximity to so many expatriates. Indeed, I found my experiences enabled me to work in a way that narrowed the differences among the various cultures in our company communities. As time has passed, I have continued to appreciate the role expatriates played in the development of the company and the Kingdom and have sought to formally recognize this through driving forward the program of Saudi Arabia expatriate retiree reunions.

LESSONS FROM LEADERSHIP

From the perspective of experience, I have discovered a few important rules for dealing with employees. I have found that it is crucial to listen to their desires and needs, especially when there is competition to employ them between various companies in the area. Keeping or retaining an employee is tough as many want to shift or change for a better opportunity. Nevertheless, this should not excuse any management from considering ways and means to retain them, especially after spending time in developing and training them.

These days, it is becoming increasingly necessary for companies like Saudi Aramco to listen to their staff and consider how to give them what they are looking for. Even if a company lacks the financial means to accommodate the wishes of its employees, the employee could, for example, be enticed by guaranteed advancement within the company. Many employees would like opportunities to experience a range of work environments but most look ultimately for job stability so they can maintain a secure and comfortable lifestyle.

I believe an open-door policy should be maintained with employees. Extending one's readiness to talk with their employees conveys a great deal of comfort and boosts confidence. Try to share the decision-making process with them from time to time, to show them I am listening and value their opinions. Such communication allows the employees to feel they are part of the discussion, investing them in the task at hand. It also demonstrates the value and strength of team decision-making processes. In the end, it is important to develop an appreciation of their work and consider some kind of financial reward, but not necessarily a salary increase.

I have tried not to intervene in an employee's work unless it was absolutely necessary. Everyone makes mistakes and it is important to learn from them. While I don't like to come down hard on anyone, I do believe in taking issues seriously and allocating time to work together with the employee to reach a satisfactory result. I see people fail for a number of reasons, including a lack of willingness to consult others who may be wiser or have more experience or education. They also may give up too easily after a failure instead of demonstrating resilience and retrying.

For some years now there has been a high rate of youth unemployment in the Kingdom. Since retiring from Saudi Aramco, I have heard many businessmen complain about the failure of some of the young Saudis to commit themselves to a job or work generally. The importance of having a good work ethic is something we need to stress to our youth from an early age. My early career was governed by self-discipline and commitment; I took my work very seriously and valued any opportunities offering further education. In my time, we put up with harsh working conditions and made sacrifices. Today's youth are far less patient and much more demanding, questioning everything expected of them. They all want to be managers straight away without first truly understanding the subtleties of the businesses they want to manage.

As a result, I have come to the conclusion that it would be helpful for every young Saudi to wear uniform and serve their country in the armed forces for at least two years in order to develop a sense of responsibility and learn commitment toward his or her nation and any subsequent employer. This will help develop aptitudes such as reliable timekeeping, pride in successfully completing all the duties required under normal circumstances, as well as maintaining acceptable levels of productivity.

IN MY HUMBLE OPINION, Saudi Aramco is a vital company and plays an important role in the Kingdom. We are proud of its achievements and its investments in various parts of the wider Kingdom society. The Home Ownership program and building of model schools and clinics in nearby communities are only some of its major contributions to making the lives of its employees and other citizens more comfortable. Its support to various benevolent societies also continues to be highly valued through its donations.

Saudi Aramco showed the strength of its tenacity recently after the 2019 drone attacks on the Abqaiq refinery and facilities. Despite the devastation and the massive size of the restoration process required, regular operations were restored in record time. I express my whole-hearted admiration and believe the company has done a superb job. Commendations for their performance have also come from both local authorities and internationally for their efficiency in bringing operations back to a normal level.

I join with most of my fellow citizens in expectantly looking forward to what the Kingdom's Vision 2030 will achieve for our society, economy and future. So far, generally speaking, I have been very pleased with the ongoing new developments I observe in so many fields, such as entertainment, museums, sports, industry and technology. There are already many overall improvements and efficiencies in the ways the government itself is managing the daily business of its citizens and the expatriate workforce. Long may these changes continue!

DR. SADAD AL-HUSSEINI SHARES SOME IMPRESSIONS

I joined Aramco as a new graduate in Geology in the early 1970s. I had just gotten my Ph.D. and was in between going out to the drilling rigs and trying to settle to camp life when I met Mr. Baluchi. He was always around supervising in the community services facilities and was very friendly and helpful with solutions and advice. Ali knew everybody and was everybody's friend, expats as well as Saudis and other Asian employees.

Ali has always been a very smart and sensitive manager. I first went on an Aramco official trip with him and other associates to the Arab Petroleum Congress in Dubai in 1975. We were impressed with the casual atmosphere and the way the Emir of Dubai was hosting and mingling with the guests at a dinner reception for the congress attendees.

At a later date in the mid-1980s, Ali and I were part of a small Aramco group that attended a management retreat in Taif that was organized by the former Saudi minister of Petroleum Abdullah Turaiki and professors from the Harvard Business School. His ideas and comments were always insightful and revealing while we discussed a variety of business cases.

WHEN RETIREMENT COMES

I retired from Saudi Aramco in April 1990. My retirement citation reads:

"Your pursuit of excellence in the management of housing, recreation, maintenance, food and retail services will always be remembered alongside your strong leadership in initiating and promoting the development, training and advancement of Saudi Arab employees."

It is a citation I am proud of.

~ 15 ~

A FULFILLING
RETIREMENT

I APPROACHED MY RETIREMENT with some objectives in mind. There had been times during my career when, asked the name of my wife, I would reply "Aramco", and I regret now that my occupation so often took precedence over my family life. It is hard to break the habits of a lifetime and, even as I became engaged with new business and community interests post-Aramco, my mother continued to complain until her passing that I never had enough time for her.

Following a popular trend in retirement, I built a new house, which took me three years to complete. It is located in an area adjacent to the "white compound" where I constructed eight villas for our children about 30 years ago. This beautiful new retirement home was built with modern materials and appliances, and all the various necessary and helpful features for comfortable ageing. However, Amira and I have not yet moved into the new house as our current neighbors have pressured us to remain in our existing house. We kept trying to move for six months without success and finally decided to stay where we are and lease the other house.

I have come to believe that, while new retirees should enjoy some relaxation, they also need to develop new routines, involving themselves in a range of different activities. They also have a responsibility to continue participating in the building of their own community.

My retirement from Saudi Aramco happened in April 1990 but, as I have already intimated, it heralded a raft of new opportunities for me to explore while immersing myself in ongoing interests. While I pursued some personal business interests and sat on various boards, I also became much more involved in community and Chamber of Commerce activities — the latter requiring active membership and seats on the Retirees Committee, Tourism and Hotel Committee, and Fisheries and Agriculture Committee. All these committees shared an objective of finding the most appropriate ways to improve the lives of the employees and retirees from these industries within the Eastern Province.

SAUDI ARAMCO RETIREES ADVISORY COMMITTEE

My interest in progressing the comfort of people in retirement led me to collaborate with other Saudi retirees and former colleagues to form an Aramco Retiree Advisory Committee. Our intention was to discuss with Saudi Aramco ways and means of improving the lives and conditions of the local workforce after leaving the company. Naturally, I cleared my plan with the Saudi Aramco President, Ali Al-Naimi, prior to embarking on the project.

Over its first five-year period, this new association raised some important issues, which were then followed up by representations made to the company management. One key issue was to get approval for retirees to continue using company facilities, including the hospitals, which was quickly achieved. We also negotiated for vehicle stickers to be issued to them, thus facilitating ongoing easy access to the company's residential communities. I continue to sit on the Saudi Aramco Retirees Advisory Committee, alongside a number of other enthusiastic and committed retirees.

NATIONAL REPRESENTATION FOR RETIREES

Once again with the assistance of others, I was instrumental in seeing the formation of a National Retirement Association, with its headquarters in Riyadh and now with branches in 14 cities throughout the Kingdom. By the year 2000, a retirement club had been built in Riyadh by HRH Prince Salman bin Abdul Aziz (who is now King), with an annual membership fee of 2,000 riyals. Another was established in the Eastern Province, but a membership fee of 500 riyals was considered by locals to be too high. As a result, it was reduced to 100 riyals for associate and 300 riyals for active membership.

In a recent development, the local municipality has offered our local National Retirement Association branch a piece of land on which to build its regional headquarters. As we write, the necessary planning process is being undertaken by local design and engineering companies and it is hoped that sponsorships from other local companies will facilitate the build.

I am always interested to hear how life is progressing for my many expatriate friends who have retired back to their home countries. In September 2018, while on vacation in the United States, my wife Amira and I visited my old college friend, Addie Hudson. She picked us up from our hotel and drove us to her current home within a most pleasant community, specifically designed for those 55 years of age and older. We were impressed with the various support facilities and resources designed for making the lives of the residents more comfortable. Addie hosted us for a tasty luncheon at the dining facility before taking us on a tour of the various other facilities on offer. These excellent services included a pharmacy, clinic, games and exercise rooms, library, woodwork shop and swimming pools.

MOHAMMED SAEED AL-ALI COMMENTS ON CHANGE LEADERSHIP

Ali is a champion of change for the better. He is the grandfather of so many improvements to the benefits and privileges for the Saudi Arab retiree. Also, with Ali's diligent and persuasive efforts, the company established reunions for both male and female Saudi retirees in Dhahran, Al-Hasa and the other provinces. Such reunions continue to cement the strong ties between the company and its pioneers. The varied programs during these events are cherished by the thousands attending and each looks forward to the next occasion. These celebrations and festivities bring a lot of joy to those who worked hard and shared many work and social experiences.

As the leader of change, Ali involved many of his colleagues both within and outside of the company as well as many local businessmen in creating a winning formula for all the Saudi Arabia reunions. As a result, a number of other local companies have followed suit and started reunions for their own retirees.

GATHERINGS OF FRIENDS AND COLLEAGUES

Over the years, I have found it beneficial to encourage those in Saudi Aramco's Executive Management to meet from time to time with Saudi retirees. Men of such stature as Frank Jungers, former Chairman and CEO, have been my guest on numerous occasions in order to meet and mix with Saudi retirees in our home. Such gatherings are well-received, especially among those with work experiences or interests in developmental projects shared in common while still working for the company.

I am always pleased by how much these occasions are enjoyed by all concerned and, consequently, the retirees generally ask me when they can expect another such gathering to take place. It is often through informal conversations at such events that we can hear about concerns and issues for the retirees, as well as opportunities to catch up with the latest news.

It is not just me who understands the importance of hosting such events. For many years there has been an annual event, held during the holy month of Ramadan and hosted by the CEO in honor of the Minister of Petroleum and Mineral Resources (now the Minister of Energy). Known as the "Ghabga'h," all active and retired company executives are invited to attend this auspicious occasion, and it is always a popular event.

A successful businessman and dear friend of mine for over 30 years, Hamad Al-Salim, also organizes an event annually on the second Wednesday of each Ramadan, inviting me and many other friends to enjoy an evening of joyful fellowship and reunion. This has become a bit of a tradition now, one of the many memorable occasions among friends who celebrate together during the evenings of Ramadan. Hamad always reminds us well in advance by fax and telephone, so we don't forget the importance of our meeting at his beautiful house in Al-Khobar. I commend him for keeping up the tradition. Just like me, he loves to stay in touch with his retired friends.

I particularly enjoy the opportunity for a good discussion about global events and affairs. For instance, my opinion of the World Bank is different to that of many people I know. I feel that the best option for any country must be to manage and run its own economy without a loan from the World Bank. As soon as a government applies for a loan, the World Bank inevitably imposes controls on it and may demand changes in the country's society through these conditions or as taxes. This can lead to citizen unrest. I admire the steps taken by Dr. Mahathir Mohamad, Prime Minister of Malaysia, when he rejected the World Bank's proposals to improve his country's economy. Malaysia has chosen not to borrow from the Bank since 1999 and their relationship has been maintained on a purely knowledge-sharing basis. The Malaysian economy has remained strong, based on its ability to diversify effectively.

THE DAMMAM AGRICULTURAL COOPERATIVE

Another interest I nurtured in retirement was an association with the Dammam Agricultural Cooperative. This came about because, at the time I left Saudi Aramco, I owned a nice little farm on the way to Jubail. It was a pleasant and restful area where some of my friends, including expatriate families, would visit and enjoy their recreational time. The farm was my first wife's favorite place for spending most of the weekends with the children and our many dear friends.

The Agricultural Cooperative has a membership of about 100 farmers. Its basic role is to sustain the various needs of the farmers, such as the provision of tools and seeds, provide any necessary farming information, advice and support, and help with the marketing of its members' products. The marketing part has not succeeded so well due to lack of cooperation from the farmers, who prefer to sell their own produce.

I held the position of chairman for 20 years. Although I tried many times to step down, each new board always asked me to stay! I did eventually declare my intention to resign and was subsequently able to do so at the following general assembly. They are now hoping for some new young blood!

THE FIRST SAUDI CERTIFIED ATTRACTIONS EXECUTIVE

The International Association of Amusement Parks and Attractions (IAAPA) is a trade association for all permanently sited amusement facilities, including amusement and theme parks, water parks and resorts. After my retirement from Saudi Aramco, I worked in different capacities on the board of the Saudi Amusement Company, eventually taking on the chairmanship for nine years. I was subsequently invited to join the board of IAAPA in 2000, which required trips to the United States for meetings and the biannual family summer gathering, always held at one of the parks.

I went on to become the first Saudi to gain the designation of IAAPA Certified Attractions Executive (ICAE) for demonstrating a high level of competence and expertise in Attractions Management. I achieved this in 2011 by successfully completing all the requirements of the ICAE as they pertained to the Kingdom.

As Managing Director and Board Chairman of the Saudi Amusement Company, I oversaw projects including the development of the Corniche Fun Land, the Video Computer Center at King Fahd

Park in Dammam, and an amusement area at the Aziziyah Resort Complex. During my chairmanship, the board members were committed to providing reasonably priced entertainment, even if it meant that at times the company only broke even. In the early years, the 45 owners felt that there was more value in building amusement parks for children to enjoy than in just giving gifts or presents to them. Playing in an amusement park was also much more beneficial for their overall health and well-being.

Up until that time, only females and children were allowed to be admitted together into amusement park facilities. However, I observed a growing interest and enthusiasm from fathers who desired to accompany their wives and children to the parks as a family outing. I finally decided with another board member and prominent businessman, Sheikh Omar Khalid Alamdar, that it was time to raise the issue and discuss opening up parks for whole families to visit and enjoy together.

We brought our proposal to the Governor of the Eastern Province, HRH Prince Mohammed bin Fahd. We promised him that the necessary and adequate controls and restrictions would be established if he allowed us to proceed with the proposed changes. He accepted and approved the entrance of families to the parks. This change went on to generate additional revenue for the company and increased pleasure for families, who could now enjoy more recreational time with both parents and children all together.

I repeatedly exhorted to my various boards the necessity of regularly changing and improving the attractions on offer, because children anticipate and look forward to revisiting their favorite parks. After I stepped down, subsequent boards changed their policies and ran the parks without considering any updating or replacement of equipment or attractions. They also terminated the contracts of some key personnel. At present, the company is struggling to survive. I have lost interest in it.

SULEIMAN AL-ABDULLAH RECALLS TIME WORKING AT THE SAUDI AMUSEMENT COMPANY

In 1992 , I was the Assistant General Manager for the Saudi Amusement Company, which was suffering from losses and needed to restructure, develop and evolve. Ali Baluchi was appointed as Managing Director for the company. I had already worked for two years with the company and he liked the work that I had done so far, but his open-mindedness to industry developments helped me move forward with managing the company and, in 1994, the company turned a profit for the first time and went on to become well-known in Saudi Arabia.

Ali provided me good managerial training with Walt Disney, Warner Brothers and Magic Mountain, as well as exposure to a comprehensive program at Cornell University. Ali believed in developing human resources and improving skills.

He is a good follow-up man, supporting employees' families too, as he understands that the home is still a priority for any working man.

I have fond memories of our time working together until 1997. I continue to see and visit him frequently, ever mindful of the positive impact he had on my managerial life.

NATIONAL TOURISM COMMITTEE

An invitation came to join the National Tourism Committee, a position that would require me to attend meetings in most of the Kingdom's provinces. The objective of this group was to promote tourism and hotel developments and suggest ways to manage and improve the pilgrimage events in the Holy Cities of Makkah and Al-Madinah. My particular interest was to promote the establishment of Visitor Information Centers as a service to help tourists in important cities and areas of interest.

Within Saudi Arabia, until very recently, it was normal for friends and relatives to stay with their parents or other relatives or at a friend's house when visiting or travelling from place to place. Hotels did not become a general necessity for quite some time and were then only available in very limited supply for specific business requirements.

Some of the earliest hotels were constructed by connecting several pre-existing houses. I believe it was Abdullah Al-Khaja, a businessman from Bahrain, who opened the first hotel in Al-Khobar. However, some residents of Al-Khobar would claim that it was Ahmed Shah, another Bahraini, who became the first hotelier when he started offering rooms with an outdoor toilet and a small restaurant serving Gulf cuisine. I also recall that there was a Saudi, Mohammed Al-Matloob, who opened a 10-room hotel in the early days of Al-Khobar's development.

In the past, many of the wealthier residents of Al-Khobar would gather in the town during the evenings to drink tea and soft drinks, smoke shisha, and exchange pleasantries among themselves. Later, a general store was also constructed where American products were sold, eventually becoming a popular place among the Western expatriates. This building was then converted to a hospital and after that became the two-star Bahrain Hotel, managed by Ahmed Shah.

Subsequently, with the developments brought to the region by Aramco and its suppliers, it was necessary for more hotels to open around Al-Khobar. These included the Royal Al-Nasr, the Al-Jabir and the Al-Nimran. As the oil and other industries expanded, the need for four- and five-star hotels increased too. The Al-Gosaibi and Meridien hotels filled a large vacuum, becoming well-used and popular with many businessmen who came to Saudi Arabia to do business with the Kingdom and its companies. In the last 10 years, a number of well-known hotel chains have also established themselves in the local market, offering further choices to customers. The facilities in many of these newer hotels reflect the significant recent changes in Saudi society, particularly regarding the status of women and the increased need for many to travel for work or education. Hotels now offer women female-only gyms, designated pool hours and non-segregated dining facilities.

Being a member of the National Tourism Committee gave me some useful insight and an effective network of contacts when it came to planning the Saudi Arabia Expat Reunions. It has been gratifying to watch how tourism services have developed within the Kingdom over recent years, and that an ever-widening choice of hotels, trips and tours is now on offer both to our guests who return to visit their Kingdom home and to tourists more generally. I am also encouraged to see an increasing number of Saudi families travelling within the Kingdom for the pleasure of discovering for themselves the many treasures and richness of their own cultural heritage.

Recently, the Ministry of Tourism was tasked to investigate ways for Saudi Arabians to spend their free time more constructively. As a result, throughout the Kingdom a number of key tourist destinations were identified where a range of activities, events, offers and packages could be developed to suit all tastes, interests and budgets.

This objective was a direct response to the dreams of HRH Prince Mohammed bin Salman, the Crown Prince, as indicated in his Vision 2030 statement.

I am pleased to say that this dream is now becoming reality, with developments stretching from historical Tabuk in the north and the beautiful Red Sea beaches of Umluj and Yanbu, to the King Abdullah Economic City and Jeddah, the magnificent Sarawat mountain range, the city of Taif, the dense forests and heritage villages of Al-Baha, and the southern city of Abha.

The Ministry of Tourism is tasked with the organization, development and promotion of all aspects relating to the tourism sector in Saudi Arabia and is looking for opportunities to both enhance the sector and overcome obstacles to its growth. Research conducted by the Supreme Commission for Tourism while preparing their National Tourism Development Plan identified and evaluated more than 12,000 sites of natural and cultural interest across the Kingdom, covering a truly diverse range of environments. Tourism assets include 25 National Parks and 16 protected areas and reserves; a plethora of unique and diverse archaeological and heritage sites; a legacy of regional and traditional handicraft industries still actively employing thousands of artisans; and world-class sporting event facilities. Indeed, the Kingdom's cultural and environmental wealth offers immense potential for both domestic and international tourism growth, in areas including diplomacy; business conferences and exhibitions; education and training; culture; heritage and antiquities; eco-tourism adventures; theme parks; sporting activities and events; and agriculture.

Previous residents of the Kingdom may have once bemoaned a shortage of good hotels available for travelers around the Kingdom, but this is fast becoming history as infrastructure and services are augmented in line with other developments. The goal, in cooperation with local and foreign investors and local investment funds, is to establish 500,000 new hotel rooms across the Kingdom by 2030. The absorptive capacity of the nation's airports will be increased by more than 100 million passengers annually over the same period, with the hope that the sector as a whole will create an additional 1.6 million jobs.

Saudi Arabia launched its first tourist visa in September 2019. Citizens of 49 countries are now able to receive a visa electronically, while holders of passports from the United States, the United Kingdom and the Schengen Area can receive a visa upon arrival. The 49 countries are representative of 80 percent of tourism expenditure globally, and 75 percent of the luxury tourism market. Citizens of other nations are able to apply through their local Saudi embassy.

I am particularly excited about some of the larger projects and I am hoping they will be completed by the time of our next in-Kingdom Aramco Annuitants Reunion in 2023. These unique offerings include the Diriyah Gate north-west of Riyadh, which will become one of the world's lifestyle destinations for culture and heritage, hospitality, retail and education; and Al-Ula, a world heritage site near Al-Madinah known for its natural beauty and pristine archaeology, currently being developed into the globe's largest living outdoor museum by French agency Afalula.

The largest project is known as NEOM. Managed by a former Saudi Aramco executive, Nadhmi Al-Nasr, NEOM aims to boost the pace of economic development in Saudi Arabia. It will include the development of towns and cities, ports and enterprises, entertainment venues and tourist destinations. It will also be the home and workplace of a million citizens from around the world.

This independent economic zone will be powered solely by renewable energy, spanning three countries (Saudi Arabia, Jordan and Egypt) complete with autonomous laws and regulations and all strategically designed for economic stimulation. NEOM is a pillar of Saudi Vision 2030.

These are exciting times for Saudi citizens as our nation opens up to the global community, providing so many opportunities for the future of our young people and society generally. A very different approach to my time on the National Tourism Committee!

THE AMERICAN SAUDI DIALOGUE FORUM

I recently encountered a new book entitled "Saudi International Relations: Lobbying as a Model," written by Dr. Ibrahim Al-Mutrif, in which he discusses a variety of ways and means to spread general but more accurate knowledge about the Kingdom to outside interests. He presents a model for achieving this. His basic idea is to strengthen the role of lobbying for a more positive view of Saudi Arabia within the United States, focusing on methods that include not only lobbying but also soft diplomacy and discussion forums, and stressing the importance of friendship in order to help bolster the Kingdom's reputation in the world. He even suggests the hiring of writers, diplomats and lawyers specifically to combat the arguments of those deliberately trying to slander the Kingdom.

Dr. Al-Mutrif is a close friend of mine. He has initiated the concept of an American Saudi Dialogue Forum, an idea I am very supportive of and have encouraged him to pursue. While there seems to be a general acceptance of the concept among the Americans he has approached, the blessing of the Saudi government for such an undertaking is still being sought, and Dr. Al-Mutrif continues to engage enthusiastically in discussing his vision with them.

I took it upon myself to introduce the concept of the forum to several groups of Saudi Aramco annuitants. I received a wide degree of acceptance and appreciation for it, especially as it is first intended to cement the historical relationship between Saudis and Americans. Since there continues to be an absence of genuine dialogue between the two nations at many levels, the concept is to link this forum to an institution that will help to enable and sustain an enlightened educated and scientific dialogue.

The forum has many objectives, such as fostering and spreading knowledge and cultural awareness, as well as providing tools and platforms for the resolution of perceived differences or conflicts. The formal establishment of such an organization is becoming an increasing necessity in a changing political climate where the continuity of an historically well-defined and concrete friendship between two countries is so clearly under threat. My hope is that the forum will be implemented without further delay and become more than just an optimistic plan.

MUHAMMED A. TAHLAWI COMMENTS ON THE NATIONAL ASSOCIATION OF RETIREES

Mr. Baluchi's remarkable bonding efforts with his friends and acquaintances, and his sincere care for them, are probably the most impressive traits of his truly inspiring personality. Not only did these particular characteristics make him a legend among all Aramcons but also a magnet and a pivotal catalyst in any gathering of old Aramco workmates, whether organized and held in Saudi Arabia or elsewhere in the world. You can ask any Aramco retiree about who they would most remember from their reunions, and I bet the answer you will receive from most, if not all of them, will be "Ali Baluchi."

This great personal characteristic was also embodied in his efforts to establish a national organization for retirees in Saudi Arabia. He and a few of his colleagues struggled for a good number of years until they were able to establish a "Retirees Committee" through the Eastern Province Chamber of Commerce and Industry. But he did not stop there. He continued his efforts until a full[y]-fledged National Association of Retirees was established.

Mr. Baluchi's enduring legacy can be summed up in what I see as three admirable aspects of his character:

1. He has a sincere love and care for those around him, especially his old friends and colleagues, and his constancy in gathering them together. He fully enjoys and is proud of such gatherings.

2. His impressive ability to reconcile different views and opinions and to lead discussions among opposing parties to reach a common unifying objective.

3. He possesses a genuine willingness to lead efforts to help and assist others in his social or business community. This was clearly demonstrated in those collaborative efforts with his colleagues that culminated in the establishment of the National Retirees Association.

16

AN ENDURING PASSION

SOCCER, A BEAUTIFUL GAME, has been a lifelong interest of mine.

The discovery of oil and gas impacted life for everyone living in this secret land, heralding both better standards of living and exposure to a wider range of activities. Soccer grew in popularity in the region starting in 1938 with the arrival of different nationalities coming to work the oilfields. The passion of the expats for playing their sport spread quickly throughout Aramco with facilities being provided for employees to use, and very soon Saudi clubs also began to appear in Al-Khobar, Dammam and other parts of the Kingdom from 1939 and 1940 onwards. Soon, large groups of children could be seen on every street kicking a ball around, myself included.

One particular incident from the 1950s serves to illustrate my colorful and somewhat passionate relationship with the sport. During a soccer event held in Aziziyah, I was playing with the local Al-Khobar squad playing against an Italian team. It was a lively game, but at one point, one of the Italian players pushed me down so hard and fast that I retaliated by hitting him. The game stopped and the police were called. They took me to the nearby Police Station and placed me under something like house arrest, perhaps to calm down the situation. However, the Al-Khobar spectators insisted they would not return back to Al-Khobar without me and the police were finally forced to release me.

I was not as good a player as I would have liked to be. Consequently, I quickly shifted to administrative work within the club and became the Team Secretary. In the early days, we held our meetings in somebody's home in order to organize and run the team's activities. After a few years, however, it became easier to rent houses to use as our club base.

The popularity of the sport continued to build momentum, but it was not until the early 1970s that the Government saw the need to begin constructing facilities for major clubs in larger cities around the Kingdom. This initiative resulted in facilities for one club being built in Al-Khobar and two constructed in Dammam.

One drawback of my trips to the United States to study was that my involvement with local soccer had to be put on hold for that period of time. I should mention, however, that I volunteered as a sports reporter for some time, writing and commentating on the local sport for an Aramco publication, the weekly *Oil Caravan*.

During the 1960s, my local club was named Al-Shua'lah. I became the club's Executive Vice President and an Al-Khobar businessman named Sheikh Abdul Aziz Al-Gosaibi was selected as President. Later in the decade, in 1967, the Shua'lah club was merged with the other local soccer teams to create a unified club in Al-Khobar known as Al-Qadisiyah. I was elected by representatives from all the different teams as the very first President of Al-Qadisiyah Sports and Social Club. It was a four-year appointment, beginning from 1967. Many great statesmen then followed me into the position, including my dear friends Saif Husseini, Ahmed Al-Zamil, Fahd Al-Hazza, Ali Badgheesh, Jasim Al-Yagoot and Abdul Aziz Al-Houty to name but a few.

When Prince Faisal bin Fahd was in charge of sports in the Kingdom, he visited our club. I took the opportunity to ask him if it would be possible to buy a large piece of land in Al-Khobar, known then as the Yacoub Field, to provide a location for a future facility for the Al-Qadisiyah Club. His Highness was very amenable to the suggestion and touched his index finger to his nose, thereby declaring his agreement.

The early days of our soccer club were challenging — we were not well-organized or well-financed, members were reluctant to pay membership dues and players even had to share soccer shoes. However, I am pleased to say that our perseverance and diligence paid off and Al-Qadisiyah became a role model for other clubs and for the behavior of young people generally. Our vision was to raise well-educated and culturally mature young people within our club and our methods even included hiring an English language teacher to teach classes on the roof of our building during the evenings. We helped our players to set goals for personal improvement whilst providing any support they needed to enhance their performance.

Not only did we have a full program of soccer games operating within the Saudi National League, but we also developed a program of various other sports, social and cultural events. This helped to build a sense of community and contributed significantly to the overall success of the club. To help overcome some of our financial challenges, we invited support from local retirees at a rate of 500 riyals year. Also, every six months we held an event to which we invited local businessmen so that they could meet our players and young people with a view to offering support and sponsorship. We also managed to retain the support of some of the local families responsible for founding the early soccer clubs, families such as that of Hamid Obaidly.

As the years passed, however, my experience as the first club president and as a board member meant my skills and knowledge continued to be called on whenever the club faced challenging times. One such period occurred between 2011 and 2012 when, through poor board leadership, an imbalance was caused by a shift to focus only on the soccer. The leadership had become less than transparent, resulting in a number of major problems. These included the chairman not consulting other board members over major decisions; little clarity about club finances, as funds disappeared without explanation and payments to meet regular obligations were late; lack of discussion about the hiring of expensive players; infrequent board meetings; and some players even being threatened. I was also concerned that the number of matches being played had reduced and that there was a distinct decline in participation by the membership.

Elections only served to accentuate these issues. Things became so heated that one member was even expelled for cursing the board members. What the club needed was stability and to be positively reunited in membership.

I was called upon to take a lead as mediator. I endeavored to encourage club members to consider how they could improve the club across all areas: management, social and cultural profile and fostering loyalty. We held meetings where we discussed the issues and how they might be resolved. Finally, with the support of five others within the leadership, I wrote to the Governor of the Eastern

Province to explain our difficulties and to ask for his support in approaching the Ministry for Youth for an independent investigation into matters in order to avoid potential further internal conflict.

Once more, in 2013, I found myself in the local press exhorting the club membership to renew its engagement and support. I asked for the membership to reach a swift consensus over the club's leadership, so that its welfare could be the primary goal and further conflict avoided. I believe strongly that sports should bring people together, not divide them, and I have always given my help and support towards that end.

I was thrilled when one of the club's Ramadan Leagues was named after me in 2017. This is a popular time for leagues to be played and it was wonderful to see so many young people enjoying the sport. I was pleased to join the players on the field at the end of the long evening to present the trophies. I was also honored when I myself was presented with an award recognizing my long service to the club and the sport.

In 2018, 20 clubs participated in the Sheik Ali Baluchi League over a 17 day period. Once again, I was pleased to see so many young people participating, and I know it has a lasting benefit on the development of the club. Another league was held in 2019, giving me an important vehicle by which to support and follow the fortunes of my club.

The Al-Qadisiyah professional soccer team has experienced somewhat of a roller-coaster ride in its recent fortunes, enjoying success within the highly competitive atmosphere of the premier league with the strongest clubs and then dropping down to the lowest league before returning back to the top and, most recently, dropping right down again in 2019-2020. This has not been helped by a raft of administrative problems, including overspending when purchasing expatriate players that weren't used to the club bureaucracy. We do not need lots of expats in the club — it is much better to train and teach the Saudi youth. I really wonder how much was achieved by the acquisition of six expatriate players, particularly when the club had to sell a group of its Saudi players to other clubs to meet financial obligations.

For as long as I am able, I will continue my interest in the club as a fan and supporter — it has become an integral part of my daily life. I especially enjoy following and watching the games and I appreciate the club's current role in building a local sports academy.

M. A. TAHLAWI REMEMBERS GETTING INVOLVED WITH THE AL-QADISIYAH CLUB

In 1979, I attended a meeting of the General Assembly of Al-Qadisiyah Club, a sports, cultural and social club. It was here that I met Mr. Baluchi and discovered that he was actively involved in public and community work in Al-Khobar. He had been the first Chairman of the Board of Directors of Al-Qadisiyah after its establishment in 1967.

I had just graduated from university and some of my colleagues had asked me to put in my papers for nomination to the upcoming Board of Directors of the club. I had already heard of Mr. Baluchi, but, in the meeting, I noticed the overwhelming respect and appreciation club members and management extended to him. The many years that passed after that showed me why he deserved all that respect and love.

Due to a minor technicality, I did not become a member of the club's Board of Directors. However, my friends, who made up the board insisted that a number of nominees, including myself, form a board support team and, as such, I was able to serve the club for several years after that.

Between 1979 and 1982, Mr. Baluchi visited the club often and attended many of the activities we organized, giving me a closer look at the superior merits of his personality. In 1982, I moved from my government job to join what is now Saudi Aramco. There, Mr. Baluchi was General Manager of Community Services. Although our career paths did not cross often, as we worked in two different organizational parts of the giant oil company, I still kept hearing rather great things about him as a person, professional and a leader.

17

A LIFETIME OF FRIENDSHIPS

AS PREVIOUSLY MENTIONED, there now exists for Saudi nationals a company-endorsed committee that acts as a representative platform for the interests and views of the organization's retirees. Its principal function is to share their aspirations and wishes with Saudi Aramco management in the expectation of receiving a reasonable and timely response.

Saudi Aramco's retired expatriate employees do not enjoy quite the same level of direct ongoing connection and communication. However, from very early on in the company's American history, it was clear that an exceptional bond of friendship developed and continues to exist between those who are associated with Aramco, although often at different times and in different ways.

The desire to nurture and continue a post-retirement connection initially generated the establishment of a company-sponsored quarterly publication titled *Al-Ayyam Al-Jamilah*, which means "Pleasant Days." The content of this magazine offered the opportunity to catch up with company news but mostly focused on items of direct interest to retirees, such as the sharing of treasured memories, contact information, ideas about what to do in retirement and cultural articles of interest to those who had lived in the Middle East.

Al-Ayyam Al-Jamilah became the catalyst and a marketing mechanism for the establishment of biannual annuitant reunions in the United States. These get-togethers (also popularly known by the Arabic word *hafla*, meaning "party") were motivated by the desire to revisit and share those many unique experiences of living and working in the Kingdom. Presenting an opportunity to renew old friendships and share memories attracted a large number of attendees. Each event was (and still is) organized by a few or team of enthusiastic volunteers with varying degrees of official support from the company.

After each reunion, *Al-Ayyam Al-Jamilah* would usually publish a special edition full of news, memories and photographs of attendees, generating further enthusiasm for belonging within the Aramco family. This tradition continues to this day, although the publication content now reflects a much more global Saudi Aramco family, with a regular program of retiree reunions being promoted in other nations including Canada, the United Kingdom, India and Pakistan. A plethora of more informal and localized gatherings are also held regularly around the world, from lunch clubs to golf tournaments. These tend to reflect more of the cultural backgrounds of the local retirees but are clearly driven by the desire to stay connected within the company family.

Throughout my working life, circumstances brought me into daily contact with the company's expatriate communities and created many opportunities to share in the lives of those who had come to join Saudi Aramco from overseas. For me, with my natural curiosity and affinity for people, it was a valuable learning environment, providing me with a significant cultural exposure and a large circle of friends. The minute I became interested in community affairs, I also found myself wanting to attend the retiree reunions in the United States. I believe I have attended most of them since the first bi-annual event held in California back in 1958. I find the reunions a pleasant way to cement friendships with the people who physically and mentally helped us build our country, and I continue to feel indebted to them in so many ways. I can also claim that photos of me have appeared regularly in *Al-Ayyam Al-Jamilah* as a result!

THE FIRST ARAMCO ANNUITANT REUNION

Held at the Castlewood Country Club in Pleasanton, California in September 1958, the first United States reunion proved to be a runaway success. With its three golf courses and Olympic-sized swimming pool, the venue would set the standard for all similar events that followed. The location was billed as being "a spot that would be convenient to the greatest number," because at that time many of Aramco's retirees had settled close to Oakland, California, near the heartland of Standard Oil, Aramco's parent company.

Some 147 people attended this first reunion, most travelling from the West Coast, but with representation also from Saudi Arabia, Bahrain, Beirut, The Hague, New York, Missouri and Oklahoma. They included those whose careers had been with Aramco, Bapco, Tapline, SoCal and Bechtel; families, couples and singles; some who were still working, and most poignantly, widows of former employees who had passed on.

Unable to attend, Aramco's Chairman, Fred Davies, sent his best wishes from Saudi Arabia for the success of the gathering, acknowledging that "friendships founded during the early operations in Arabia are no small thing and perish the thought they should become lost." My sentiments entirely!

THE "BRAT" REUNIONS

Since 1995, another notable and popular reunion has been held regularly in the United States for company "brats" (children of expatriate Saudi Aramco employees who were born and/or grew up in the company's communities). The unique nature of this group's formative shared experiences is often forgotten or overlooked, but for so many of them, the Kingdom holds a special place in their hearts as the place they first — and still — call home. These days, it may have become more of a "virtual" home, but it is so much a part of their lives that, as the 2019 Brat Reunion brochure suggested, "Who else but another Brat could remember things like watching the sun rise over the jebels, shopping trips to al-Khobar, sunset picnics at Half Moon Bay ... and feeling that blast of heat as you stepped off the airplane and knowing you are finally 'home'?"

I watched so many brats grow up, and I know how important the Kingdom is to them. I see in our association with the brats an avenue of great opportunity to cement a realistic friendship between Saudis and Americans in which to create a long-lasting friendship and understanding. It is pleasing that the changing approach towards tourism within the Kingdom will allow more brats to revisit and reconnect with their first home.

Some brats seek to return to their old Aramco environment by gaining employment with the company, and we have a number of second and third generation brats currently living and working in the Kingdom. Many offer their help as volunteers with the in-Kingdom reunions and they are a valuable resource on the team as they have an innate understanding of the emotional attachment held by many of our returning annuitants and their families. Our brat volunteers know exactly the kinds of experiences and opportunities our guests will most appreciate in their journey to reconnect with their past, while at the same time being able to contextualize it for them against the backdrop of a modern and rapidly changing Kingdom.

I never tire of hearing my friends' excitement and pleasure at being able to "return home" to Saudi Arabia. I am always interested in the range of reactions: for some, it is confronting to see all the changes as they struggle to identify their old haunts, but for the majority they are pleased to see progress for the better and appreciate the higher quality of lifestyle choices on offer. But now I am getting ahead of myself!

While attending the 1998 reunion in Scottsdale, Arizona, I was approached privately by a number of annuitants, led by Doug Rines, who asked me, "Ali, how soon before a retiree reunion can be held in Saudi Arabia?" Pleased at their interest in returning to the Kingdom, I thought quickly, made an executive decision, and came back with a favorable response. Later that weekend, I made an announcement to the larger group of reunion attendees that the first expatriate reunion, or "KSA Reunion," in Saudi Arabia would be held in March 2000, and immediately everybody stood and applauded most enthusiastically.

Consequent to that announcement, the first thing I did upon my return to Dhahran was to arrange a meeting with Mr. Khalid Al-Falih, then Saudi Aramco's Senior Vice President of Industrial Relations. I presented to him the idea of holding an expatriate retiree reunion within the Kingdom and he immediately approved the idea. He called Mustafa Jalali, Vice President of Public Affairs, and asked him to set the process in motion.

The following week, I met with two local businessmen who were also good friends, Abdul Aziz Al-Turki and Abdul Aziz Al-Turaiki, and shared with them the concept of the expatriate gathering. They also welcomed and appreciated the notion. As they were close friends of the Deputy Governor of the Eastern Province, Prince Saud bin Naif, we called for a meeting with him too. He embraced the idea and warmly encouraged us to continue with our plans. He also agreed to persuade the Ministry of Interior to sponsor the visas for the visitors in order to more easily facilitate their participation.

It then became necessary to bring together an organizational team. It was important that this team include a mix of Saudis and expat employees, volunteers and local businessmen to start building a program for the event.

Once we decided on March 11, 2000 as the official start date, we called for expressions of interest from the retirees themselves and began compiling a list of potential attendees. It did not take long. At that time, many tasks were still performed manually, and the retirees' applications and registration fees were received by mail from their different countries of residence. I recall paying a visit to Saudi Aramco's Nassir Nafissi and asking him to provide at least 600 gifts for the reunion attendees.

Securing visas became our biggest challenge. Soon after we had provided the list of the 400 interested retirees to Prince Saud bin Naif, the principal supporter of the event, he was reassigned as the Saudi Ambassador to Spain. Prince Saud took his administrative assistant, Mohammed Al-Mutlaq, along with him, creating a problem for us in following up on the progress of the visa applications, as we no longer had an effective channel of communication into the office of the Deputy Minister of the Ministry of Interior. It then transpired that the "visa file" had temporarily disappeared, but it was difficult to call Prince Saud or his assistant to get help with locating it.

After two frustrating months of pursuing various departments at the Ministry of Interior, we managed to locate the file through the help of Saudi Aramco's Manager of Government Affairs in Riyadh, who moved the file to the Ministry of Foreign Affairs. Once then-Crown Prince Abdullah bin Abdul Aziz approved the issuing of visas to the annuitants through Saudi Arabia's global network of embassies and consulates, the Foreign Ministry then had to more directly inform and instruct all of the Kingdom's consulates in the countries where the annuitants resided.

The retirees began applying for visas, cognizant that they had to pay the fees themselves. It was their responsibility to contact and then travel to the various consulates, but for some the experience was less than smooth, with a distinct lack of cooperation from consulate staff; applicants were frequently told that their names were not listed on the message from the Foreign Ministry. Fortunately for them and us, each name had also been assigned a serial number and a designated consulate on the original list.

It fell to me to call the Foreign Ministry and each of the consulates involved to ensure the names of the annuitants were on the correct lists, providing the serial number when necessary. This communication was all done through fax and landline. Consequently, the whole process of issuing the visas took a lot longer than expected.

These delays were disheartening for everyone involved, especially our planning team, who at times worried that some annuitants would be unable to make their historic journey back to Saudi Arabia. We did actually lose one team member in the process, but I was able to persuade the rest to continue on with the mission. Since this was the first reunion in Saudi Arabia, it was important to have a motivated team to invest the time needed to discuss and plan our potential program with the various interested organizations.

In the end, due to the visa hiccups, history was made on April 18 when the group of about 300 retirees plus a few brats joined us in Saudi Arabia for the event. Although we started several weeks later than anticipated, the overall feedback from attendees indicated that it was a huge success.

For me, the event was the realization of my long-held dream of being able to return the hospitality offered to me so generously at so many of the reunions I had attended in the United States. I was also incredibly appreciative and proud of the considerable enthusiasm we had been able to muster in support of this first official gathering on Saudi soil. I remember we also had considerable help from the 100 or so brats working for Saudi Aramco at that time.

The success of this reunion laid the foundations for the subsequent gatherings following in 2009, 2015 and 2019. We established an event structure that proved to be a winning formula for all concerned. We still follow this formula for each new event, and it includes:

- the provision of a core hospitality venue or "Reunion House" within the Dhahran community. This is used as a meeting place or focus point where team members and guests can interface on a daily basis;
- a full and diverse program of events, activities and trips both within the company's communities and facilities as well as the wider Eastern Province and Kingdom;

- reliable and comfortable transportation and accommodation;
- opportunities to explore how the company and Kingdom have developed and changed over the decades and to reconnect with people and locations of personal interest;
- a welcome banquet hosted by Saudi Aramco's CEO;
- a welcome reception hosted by the Governor of the Eastern Province;
- an energetic team of volunteers on hand to help with hospitality, information and leading trips;
- the ongoing recording of the event for company publications and archives.

Local businessmen played a key role in the early KSA Reunions by hosting some of the special events and financially sponsoring some others to help keep costs down for the guests. As I recall, the Farewell Luncheon in 2000 was held in Al-Khobar and it was several local businessmen who footed the bill. Because the dinner was a mixed event, attended by both males and females together, we had to ask the Governor, Mohammed bin Fahd, to provide special security to guard the area for the duration. It was also necessary to persuade the Moral Committee to refrain from making any interruptions! Ultimately, it was a very well-organized event, well-received and immensely enjoyed by all the annuitants and their families.

In a speech given at the official opening dinner of the 2000 KSA Reunion, Saudi Aramco's then President and CEO, Abdullah S. Jumah, warmly welcomed the retirees back to their desert home. He pointedly acknowledged "how deeply roots can go in the span of one's career". He also recognized how the effort they had made to travel to Saudi Arabia not only reflected their curiosity but was "a tribute to the worldwide fraternity of former employees."

Jumah's comments reflect my own observations of how deeply Saudi Aramco's expat employees and their families feel their connection to the Kingdom, even many years after they have left, and the energy with which they continue to seek out others who have shared the Aramco experience. Nearly twenty years on, at the 2019 KSA Reunion welcome dinner, CEO and host Amin Nasser reiterated this feeling of "extended family" by describing the Aramco family as "linked not by bloodlines, but by shared experiences... a special family... that has created an ongoing legacy."

At his own reception for the reunion guests in 2000, the Governor of the Eastern Province encouraged them not to consider the region as their second home: "Think of it as your first home," he insisted. He went on to say that he considered all of them — whether American, British, Indian, Pakistani or Dutch — "un-appointed ambassadors for Saudi Arabia." This role cannot be underestimated in our modern world and continues to lend justification to hosting reunion gatherings of expats within our rapidly changing Kingdom. As the Kingdom currently opens its borders to tourism, the KSA Reunions have also provided a captive audience with which to experiment and try out locations and itineraries and ultimately provide the very best form of publicity and marketing — word of mouth.

Hosting that first KSA Reunion gave me a great deal of personal pleasure as I welcomed back many of my old friends to Saudi Arabia, including Mrs. Elli Beckley. Some 55 years earlier, between 1950 and 1952 when she was facilitating Advanced Clerical Training, I had been one of her students at the Dhahran Industrial Training Center. She was known as Elli Keenan until she married fellow

Aramcon Jack Beckley in 1953. She fondly remembered many of her former students, including Abdullah Busbait, Abdul Majeed Al-Jamid and Ali Al-Naimi. Sadly, there are fewer and fewer of the real "old-timers" still alive or physically able to return to visit us in the Kingdom.

While Ali has many skills and abilities that explain his successes throughout life, perhaps the most significant among them is his ability to build and maintain a large network of relationships—and indeed friendships—with Aramco's international staff and retirees. Over the decades that vast global network has allowed Ali to act as a sort of conduit or bridge between these individuals, wherever they live now and regardless of when they worked for the company.

But Ali also serves as a link to the past — what retirees refer to as al-ayyam al-jamilah or "the beautiful days" spent living and working in the Kingdom. The older we get the more beautiful those days seem, and Ali has played an invaluable role in keeping precious memories and priceless friendships alive for countless Aramcons.

H.E. ALI AL-NAIMI, ADVISOR TO THE ROYAL COURT
(FORMER MINISTER OF PETROLEUM
AND MINERALS, 1995–2016)

FOR PEGGY J. SMITH, THE WELCOME MATTERS!

What most impressed me about Ali was the way he greeted everyone in a friendly manner and made all of

*us feel so welcome in his country! This has continued to
be true throughout the years he has attended reunions
in the United States, and in his role as the "ringleader"
in getting reunions started back in Saudi Arabia. He just
doesn't tire of his friends!*

A further nine years passed before we held the second KSA Reunion, largely due to various local and international security issues. In 2009, we had a stronger support team, expanded program and were able to welcome 500 retirees, brats and their families. My guiding principle, then as now, was to ensure that the visitors found or rediscovered those things most meaningful to them about Saudi Arabia, bearing in mind the context of a dynamically changing company and Kingdom.

This time, it was Khalid Al-Falih who welcomed the guests in the position of company President and CEO. He thanked them for their ongoing legacy of values and corporate culture put in place during their many years of service and likened Saudi Aramco to a tapestry where each employee and their family members were threads woven into a whole, creating a very unique company.

Al-Falih said, "Whatever job you did, whether you were a geologist, engineer or an administrator, a doctor, nurse or teacher, you played an essential role in our day-to-day operations. Family members, too, made a vital contribution, providing the support needed to help our people do their important work, making our communities vibrant, diverse, fun places to live."

He introduced the analogy of a tapestry saying, "If you think of Saudi Aramco as a tapestry, it's easy to see what I mean. It doesn't matter when the thread was woven in; it becomes an integral part of the whole, adding strength, beauty and texture. That thread's contribution is enduring and vital to the success of an enterprise crucial in the global energy equation."

Similar sentiments were expressed in 2015 when a further 600 retirees were welcomed back to the company and the Kingdom. For the third time, it was the warmth of the welcome each received and the tremendous hospitality they experienced from the company and wider Saudi community that were rated as the highlight of their visit. I found that most satisfying.

With 600 guests, we needed an effective team, and in 2015 we were blessed with more than 100 volunteers from the company and community to help keep the guests busy and comfortable. We had much positive feedback from the volunteers themselves regarding how much they had enjoyed the experience of meeting the "old-timers."

KATHLEEN "BERNI "WRIGHT RECALLS GETTING THE KSA REUNIONS OFF THE GROUND

In early 1999, Ali attended a Saudi Aramco Employees' Association meeting in Dhahran to ask for support for the first KSA Reunion. Initially, the SAEA Board didn't offer any help as some felt retirees were wealthy enough and shouldn't be given free events by the Employees Association! I felt sorry for Ali and approached him after the meeting to introduce myself. I told him I had events experience, including expanding the SAEA trips program to include day and weekend trips, organizing itineraries and attending all of the trips as tour leader myself (plus recruiting reliable tour leaders, expats and

Saudis). I said I would happily volunteer to help at the reunion.

After that, Ali invited me to attend the reunion planning meetings and before long I had been nominated to coordinate all reunion transport (the only Brit on the main team!). For that first reunion we had to do our day job and fit in volunteer duties afterwards, so it meant long hours, but Ali created an environment where we all wanted to work extra hard to make it happen.

I recall that Ali worked hard to convince management to support the event. We initially had trouble getting the visas in time, causing that first reunion had to be postponed indefinitely. Then, in early March, we heard visas had been issued and we had to quickly get reorganized, as the event was ultimately to be held in April. Throughout it all, Ali never gave up hope of pulling it off and if it wasn't for him it simply would not have happened.

Ali is very kind and has a genuine desire to help people of all nationalities. He's certainly a "poster boy" for Saudi Arabian hospitality at its very best!

I think being responsible for making the KSA Reunions a reality must be one of Ali's greatest legacies. There were many challenges to overcome, not only in convincing management that KSA Reunions would be a good idea but gaining support from local businessmen. Also pulling together the teams and working out logistics for bringing such large groups to the Kingdom. He works extremely hard to make things happen. His ambition

1 Photos from the Sheikh
   Ali Al-Baluchi Soccer
   Tournament held during
   Ramadan 2019. 16 youth
   teams participated
   with 'Gurnatah' from
   Dammam and won the
   trophy. The tournament
   was organized by
   Ahmed Al-Yahyaie
   and sponsored by
   local companies and
   organizations.

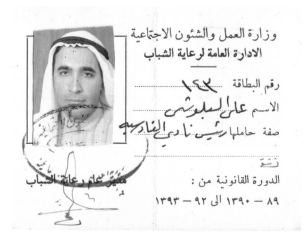

وزارة العمل والشئون الاجتماعية
الادارة العامة لرعاية الشباب

رقم البطاقة ....

الاسم علي السلوش ....

صفة حاملها رئيس نادي القادسية

الدورة القانونية من :

٨٩ — ١٣٩٠ الى ٩٢ — ١٣٩٣

1

1 One of my early membership cards from when I became President of Al-Qadisiyah Sports and Social Club.

2 Here I am receiving an Appreciation Award from HRH Prince Sultan bin Fahd, President of the Sports Authority in the Kingdom.

3 Meeting with Prince Faisal bin Fahd, who was responsible for the development of youth sports in KSA.

4 An early team photo

5 This photo includes me (the first President of Al-Qadisiyah Sportive and Cultural Club in 1967) with subsequent presidents.

2

3

4

5

6

7

6 Recently, a book
was written about
the history of the US
Consulate in Dhahran.
This page records
when I was invited
as a Guest of Honor
to the National Day
celebrations in 2014.
I am seated on the
left in the bottom
photograph.

7 Even before I retired,
I maintained strong
networks with
colleagues from
Aramco. Here I am
with Abdullah Al-Jama',
father of Nabil Al-Jama',
who was a prominent
personnel advisor at
Saudi Aramco.

8 With my fellow
problem-solving team
from the Club, known
as the 'think tank'.

9 For many years, I have
attended reunions
in the United States.
Here, catching up with
Marilyn Townsend and
her husband in Arizona,
1994. Marilyn used to
work for me in C.S. and
edited the Commissary
Matters publication.

8

1

1   Here I am welcoming 2009 Reunion guests to the Dammam Heritage Gallery (Saudi Aramco).

2   With H.E. Ali Al-Naimi.

3   CEO Jumah welcoming Reunion guests, 2000.

2

3

4

5

4   Berni Wright (left)
    excited to reconnect
    with an old colleague,
    Ed Dymicki, at the 2019
    KSA Reunion.

5   Volunteers are at
    the heart of the
    organization of the
    reunions and over 100
    helped in various ways
    both in 2015 and 2019.

6   Members of the
    2019 organizational
    committee.

6

1

2

1. At the 2009 Reunion, I had the honor of presenting HRH Prince Mohammed bin Fahd with a gift of appreciation for his ongoing support.

2. In 2019, on behalf of the Reunion, I had the honor of presenting HRH the Emir with a gift of appreciation for his ongoing support.

3. HRH the Emir of the Eastern Province Saud bin Naif bin Abdul Aziz Al-Saud greets Reunion guests in 2019.

4 An early planning
meeting of the
2019 Organizational
Committee. I am
seated between my
Vice Chairman Saeed
Al-Ghamdi and Trips
Coordinator Khalid
Al-Bubshait.

5 Reuniting with Fred
Blanchard, friend
and colleague in
Dhahran, 2015.

6 Amira and I with Munira
Al-Ashgar, a remarkable
lady who has worked
with us on each KSA
Reunion to stage events
showcasing the rich
traditions of Saudi
culture and heritage.
She also opened her
personal museum
for many tours by
our guests.

4

5

1

2

3

1 We have so many wonderful volunteers and I appreciate how seriously they take their roles. Hospitality Lead Suzanne Parmenter training in Fire Safety.

2 Volunteers Dani and Winky greet guests at the 2019 KSA Reunion welcome table.

3 Arriving at the 2015 KSA Reunion farewell luncheon with team lead Kathy Owen.

4 Aramco "Brat" Cheri Saner (second from right) was responsible for all the marketing of our later reunions; posing here in front of her 2019 Reunion House banner with her sister Michelle, fellow team members Joy Neumann, Berni Wright, Rubina Darcy and Melissa Valle.

4

5 It is good to see previous reunion volunteers returning as guests. With Valerie White and Rolie Carron in 2019.

6 2019 KSA Reunion guests showing their appreciation of Saudi Arabia while enjoying the Abha region and traditional hospitality (photo by Cheri Saner).

5

1

2

1 The Diriyah ruins near Riyadh is going to be one of Saudi Arabia's premium tourist attractions with its museums and sound and light show.

2 Retirees enjoying a trip to Madain Saleh.

3 The Nabatean tombs at Madain Saleh.

3

4

4 When Amira and I travel to attend US Reunions, we loved to visit with old friends as part of our vacation. With the Saner family, whose daughters, Michelle and Cheri, are part of our KSA Reunion planning team.

5 With Eileen and Tom Henderson in the Reunion House, 2015. Tom was active in starting the UK Reunions. We were delighted to host a celebration of their golden wedding anniversary while they were with us in Saudi Arabia as guests of the reunion.

6 A photo from the fifth and last UK Reunion hosted by the Hendersons. I am in the front row, left of center. York, 2014.

5

1

2

3

4

1. Always so many wonderful friends to catch up with in the United States!

2. Amira and I meeting up with some of my old friends and classmates from Peirce College.

3. Dear friends the Caspers, who have sponsored some of the US Reunion events I have attended.

4. Old friends Lois and Edwin Bonner who hosted me for my first Thanksgiving dinner in 1960.

5. Prominent local businessman Abdullah Fouad greets Frank Jungers in my house at a special gathering of friends.

6. Visiting Vince Quinn at his home in Los Angeles. I have always made it a priority to stay in touch with those people who have had a significant impact on my life.

5

6

1

1 Twin sisters Joyce
Kriesmer and Jackie
Larsen Voskamp meeting
King Abdul Aziz during
his 1947 visit to Aramco;
and pictured today with
relatives.

2 With 2018 UK Reunion
host team held in Bristol.

3 Larry Barnes with daughter
Laurie Getz. Larry was
in Transportation, but
I got to know him while in
Personnel, as we worked
together to resolve
employee issues. Larry
used to deliver news on
Aramco radio at 6pm
every day.

4 Dear friend Paul Case
and his wife. I knew him in
Dhahran through his work
in the Training Department
where he was a pioneer of
out-of-Kingdom training
for young Saudis.

2

3

4

5 Long-time friends, the Jupp family. Mr. Jupp was a business advisor and came to Saudi Arabia to do some work for the royal family. As a friend of the Hartzell family, we hosted him in Al-Khobar, and then subsequently stayed with each other as we travelled over the years.

6 The Parsinnen family. Jon was a professor at KFUPM and then moved to Aramco. We met through mutual friends, the Zamils and Yousefs. Jon's wife, Kathy, was actually the daughter of a friend (Floyd Teel) whom I met in 1962 when touring to recruit more international students.

7 The Rocap family. I first met the Rocap family in the 1960s in Philadelphia when they hosted me and showed me around as an international student. We have maintained our friendship through the decades.

5

6

1

1 Presenting a gift of
appreciation to our
host, Saudi Aramco
CEO Amin Nasser, at
the 2019 KSA Reunion
welcome dinner.
With my reunion
Vice-Chairman,
Saeed Al-Ghamdi.

2 Here I am with my
grandson Mishal,
Grandson Saleh, and
Granddaughter Liyan,
in Marylebone, London,
September 2018.

2

paid off, and he has made hundreds, if not thousands, of people very happy. These reunions will continue to delight others in the years to come.

If Ali had not been at the helm of the KSA Reunion Ship, it would not have sailed to port!!

(Note: Berni returned in retirement to help facilitate the planning and daily working of the 2015 and 2019 reunions.)

In 2019, a record-breaking program of more than 100 activities and trips was on offer, many illustrating how the Kingdom is developing and changing as it opens to tourism. In collaboration with Saudi Aramco's Transportation and Aviation departments, groups of reunion guests were able to experience longer visits to Abha, Asir, Riyadh and Jeddah as well as day trips to Shaybah, Al-Hasa, Mada'in Saleh and Uqair. It was a new experience for many to be on trips handled entirely by knowledgeable and helpful local Saudi guides.

Before she retired in 2009, our longtime team member Berni Wright used to lead trips for the Saudi Aramco Employees' Association, so she was particularly interested to see how this industry was developing. I was pleased when she told me that the tour companies being used by the reunion were doing a good job. She said, "They know what they are doing, and they are looking after everyone very well. It is the small touches that make the difference."

Some 60 of our reunion guests were warmly welcomed back to the Eastern Province at a reception held by Prince Saud bin Naif at his palace in Dammam. The governor expressed his sincere desire to us that the reunion guests enjoy their return to their previous home in the Kingdom and take time to rekindle their many happy memories. He also highlighted the many and great changes happening within the Saudi economy, society and community and hoped the visitors would appreciate the transformation.

The 2019 visitors were generally fascinated by the developments they observed all around them in the Kingdom. Retiree Paul Sutterlin told us, "If you come over here now, you see something that is totally different — very positive changes. There is a more of a museum milieu to experience regarding traditional Saudi culture... You don't need the same spirit of adventure that you needed coming in the '60s! I think it's a very positive thing to open up Saudi to the outside world."

The most visible change has been the progress and status of women in the work force — the teams of female guides at Ad Diriyah and Ithra, for instance, made a most favorable impression. Seeing women driving around the Kingdom was also a new experience!

I felt that the 2019 KSA Reunion deserved a five-star rating. The 11 days were greatly enjoyed by the 550 annuitants and their families, but we enjoyed their visit equally as much. The kind feedback and sincere appreciation offered by the dear visitors warmed my heart. When Ali Al-Naimi, my dear friend from childhood, asked me to carry on and manage the next reunion, I immediately agreed! Perhaps someone whispered in his ear that they thought I was stepping down!

As always, I was pleased that it was the warmth of traditional Saudi hospitality that had the biggest impact on everyone attending the reunion, with so many commenting on the kindness and generosity of the Saudi people they have met. As a result, they will most certainly be returning home as unofficial ambassadors for the Kingdom!

BILLIE TANNER ATTENDED TWO KSA REUNIONS:

It was an experience I'll never forgot going back to our other home in Saudi Arabia and reconnecting with old friends we had not seen for years. Ali was the "host with the most" — the dinners at his home were unbelievable. Such hospitality can rarely be found anywhere.

Aside from his professional persona, he will always be remembered for the KSA Reunions. His indomitable personality will undoubtedly leave a lasting impression for as long as there is sand in the Kingdom.

Operating with the blessing of the Governor of the Eastern Province is always a priority for the KSA Reunion Steering and Planning teams and one of my first jobs for each reunion is always to seek a meeting with him to gain his endorsement and guidance.

It is always a very special honor for some of our returning guests to be invited to the Governor's Palace to meet with His Royal Highness and to enjoy the warmth of traditional Saudi Arabian hospitality in his presence. We have been honored by such an occasion during each of the reunions.

Below is an excerpt from welcoming remarks made by HRH the Governor of the Eastern Province, as printed in the 2019 KSA Reunion handbook:

Ahlan wa Sahlan! It is always with the greatest of pleasure that we welcome the return of Saudi Aramco's expatriate retirees and family members to their Kingdom "home." We are most happy that you are participating in this, the fourth such gathering,

at such a significant time in our history, so you may
observe first-hand many of the important changes
that are taking place throughout our society, economy
and communities as we position ourselves to meet the
challenges for future generations.

Saudi Aramco has always played a pivotal role in
the modern development of both the Kingdom and our
cherished region. The contribution that you and your
families made during your years with the Company
can never be overestimated, and we extend our ongoing
appreciation and gratitude for the many sacrifices you
made in leaving your own countries to help further the
growth of ours.... .

HRH THE EMIR OF THE EASTERN PROVINCE,

SAUD BIN NAIF BIN ABDUL AZIZ AL-SAUD

With so many of our American friends returning to attend the KSA Reunions, it is an imperative that we also involve the United States Consulate in Dhahran in our plans for the events. I have developed pleasant and productive relationships through the years with many of the Consular-Generals assigned to the Eastern Province. In 2014, on the 70th anniversary of establishing the Consulate in Dhahran, I was invited as the guest of honor to give the address at the National Day celebrations held at the consulate. Here are some excerpts from my speech:

It has been a long time since I began my friendly
association with the US Consulate General in Dhahran.
I would guess that it all began back in the 1950s.

I still recall the day when I missed the Aramco truck that hauled employees to Dhahran for our daily work. I had to walk nine kilometers on the road and found myself passing the entrance to a construction site. Curious, I asked the workers there what was going on. Their response was "We are building American Consulate". To be truthful, I was neither aware nor familiar with the role the Consulate plays in the Eastern Province at that time, but over the years I've come to learn of the various tasks it conducts, and of the role it plays in the lives of Americans in the area (beginning with the birth certification of the Saudi born Americans who were to come).

In the 1960's I became very friendly with some of the employees of the Consulate, especially those from Bahrain — Abdullah Khamis, Ahmed, and Abdul Rahman Bubshait (although later I learned that Abdul Rahman is a Saudi citizen). In early 1960 I was selected to go to the USA to further my education, and it was necessary for me to visit the American Consulate to obtain the appropriate visas. Mr. Bubshait was working at the front desk of the visa area (receiving and issuing). He took all of my documents and, in only a few hours, I received the visa — properly stamped in my passport. I compare that to the situation today, how drastically things have changed...

The fact remains, the Consulate has played many important roles in the Eastern Province. One key role is in how the consulate has assisted many Saudi businessmen with introductions to new US commercial ventures. This at a time when the region was virgin territory, with little business activity around. With this help, business mush- roomed between USA and KSA, the business in the area becoming a classic success story.

The Consulate also builds and reinforces bilateral relationships and cooperation across many fronts, promoting a better business environment. Saudi business benefitted tremendously from the wealth of economic information the Consulate provided to local and American businessmen, narrowing the gap between them in order to achieve fruitful results. I believe the credit for this goes to the constructive role the Consulate General has played over the years in the Eastern Province, opening doors and entertaining business leaders through official and social functions at the Consulate. This forthcoming attitude by the Consulate is well recognized by the local business community as a key factor in narrowing differences and smoothing over difficulties...

The annual American Independence Day gathering at the Consulate is one of the most important events amongst the local business community, an event that it gives everyone great pleasure to attend.

This deep association with the US Consulate has helped to develop a strong love inside me for my American friends, co-workers, and others whose paths I've crossed over the year. This has led me to promote the Saudi Aramco annuitants reunion, a gathering where our expatriate Aramco colleagues can return and visit the Kingdom and see how the fruits of their efforts have prospered over the years, generating a modern Kingdom through economic and industrial development.

With the building of a new consulate, in this new century, another concrete step is being taken in cementing the relationship between the USA and the Kingdom of Saudi Arabia's citizens.

In summary, much of the investment that has led to the continuous growth of bilateral relationships and the commercial development of the Eastern Province has come about due to the constructive role played by the American Consulate here in Dhahran.

ALI M. AL-BALUCHI, 2014

MARY NORTON CONSIDERS THE IMPACT OF THE KSA REUNIONS

I'm not sure if the idea — "Why not bring them back to Saudi Arabia for a reunion?" — was solely his, but it obviously struck a note. Given the entry restrictions and other inhibiters, it must have seemed to many as impossible as it was audacious. So, of course, it had to happen. As you well know, over the years Ali has spearheaded preparations for the first of many trips "home" for ex-Aramcons and their families.

Everyone I know who made such a trip has come back with wings on their feet, thrilled and grateful for an unforgettable experience. When I learned of the plans for yet another reunion in the Kingdom in 2019, I could not believe Ali would still be willing to serve, in effect, as CEO. I'm not sure of his age (not sure he is, either) but I do know that for most of us, energy levels

are not the same as in days of yore. Where does this
energy come from? Ali will say he draws energy from
the people he meets.

JULIE EVELAND WORKED ON THE
2015 KSA REUNION:

I was invited to a reunion planning meeting in the spring
of 2014 and became part of the organization team for the
2015 KSA Reunion in Dhahran.

The reunions held around the world are important
to the lives of Aramcons but returning to the Kingdom is
a dream and a desire that many hold dear. Ali Baluchi
recognizes that and enables those dreams and desires to
come true for hundreds of annuitants and their families
at each reunion. One of the most impressive things to me
about Ali is not only his remarkable generosity and desire
to accommodate returning annuitants, but his ability
to inspire others to come together to organize and serve
to make that happen.

KATHLEEN OWEN CREDITS THE "UNWAVERING
VISION" BEHIND THE KSA REUNIONS

The KSA Reunions provide the opportunity for expats
who thought they would never see their Saudi Arabia
"home" again the chance to return for a visit. Working
with Ali on the reunion initiative, I came to appreciate
his unwavering vision. Although initially it was a
challenge to convey the "big picture," as well as the

projected long-term benefits to the decision makers, Ali's determination to persevere made the reunions a reality. The first group returned home to Saudi in 2000, with additional reunions following in 2009, 2015, and 2019. I was by Ali's side every step of the way for three of those events, planning, coordinating events, and managing logistics for the special visitors' itinerary. It was indeed so heartwarming to see Ali honored by all as the great host behind these visits, which meant so much to all who participated. Ali brought thousands of people together, to his home and to their home.

Ali possesses a true gift for bringing together people together. It is his love for his friends (worldwide) and country that spurred him to make the vision of the reunions a reality. His vision continues to produce ambassadors for the Kingdom. Former Aramcons and their families gather from around the globe to uncover the treasures and secrets of Arabia, once again discovering what we all love most about the Kingdom, notably its people, their culture, and the spirit of the desert. The visitors take those unforgettable experiences back home with them and share with others what an amazing country Saudi Arabia is, especially because of people like Ali.

I would like to take this opportunity to comment on my friendship with the Owen family, as it extends back over many years. I very much appreciated having Kathy to work at my side on the KSA Reunions, as well as all the other family members who helped in various capacities as required. After Tom's retirement, we very much missed her local input to the 2019 team, but at least she was still able to help from Houston. We were very pleased that the family returned for the reunion itself. It seemed somehow very appropriate that the 2019 Reunion House was previously the Dhahran home of Paula and Dave Owen, creating fond and poignant memories of times together in Kingdom.

I should also mention that in February 2015, Kathy and I were invited by Saudi Aramco to attend a special ceremony on behalf of the reunion team. We were among 11 individuals and five teams who were presented with awards marking excellence in the delivery of services within the company. It was an honor to be recognized in this way for services to our expatriate retirement community.

CHERI SANER ON ALI'S QUICK ADOPTION OF NEW TECHNOLOGY

One day we met at the golf course for lunch. Ali wanted to make note of our conversation and pulled out a pen and a small homemade notepad of scrap paper with a staple in the top corner — we joked that it was his version of an iPad. As Ali has always been open to learning new things, the following year he bought an Apple iPad and was soon on social media and had a personal email address. In the beginning, as he was getting familiar with using his iPad, he would call me for technical help, and I would walk him through how to fix his issues. It was endearing to see technology through his eyes and inspiring to see how he was always open to discovering new things.

MARY NORTON SHARES SOME
REUNION LORE

Ali's efforts to affirm and expand good relations between ex-Aramcons and Saudis are legendary: Many consider him to be the quintessential "goodwill ambassador." When reflecting on their time in Saudi Arabia, it is no secret that most ex-Aramcons have cherished their years and experiences, but, as time goes by, memories tend to fade. That is where Ali comes in. His presence at reunions reminds us of our connections to the company, the country and our Saudi friends.

The last we saw Ali was at the KSA Reunion near Austin in September 2018. He seemed to be everywhere at once, ubiquitous. At our first dinner, a "Chuck Wagon" affair, we were encouraged to don western duds. Ali turned up in jeans, shirt, bandana and a huge white cowboy hat. As he strolled among the tables, greeting everyone, I suspect he was meeting many for the first time. He doesn't seem to view people he hasn't met as strangers but rather as soon-to-be friends. Reunions are clearly important to him.

One of Ali's strongest traits is his ability to "make it happen." A couple of years ago, Ali and Amira were visiting friends in Georgetown, Texas, about 30 miles from Austin. He sent word to one of my retiree friends that we were invited to an evening party at the home of his hosts. Us widows of a certain age tried to figure out how we could make it to Georgetown, but with none of us driving at night, and all of us scattered about Austin, we regretfully declined. Ali came back with, "Then we will come to Austin!" We quickly revisited the issue and realized we could pull off a luncheon and invite others he knew. It turned out to be a delightful affair, not just for Ali and Amira, but for all of us who do not see one another often as in times past. Incidentally, Amira scored a big hit at the luncheon and an even bigger hit at the reunion where she drove a tour boat on Lake Austin, at least part of the way.

(Mary first settled in Saudi Arabia as a "bachelorette" in 1958, and, in 1961, married Howard Norton, a teacher at the Industrial Training Center (ITC). They retired from Aramco in 1988.)

TAM DELL'ORO COMMENTS ON
HOW TO WORK THE CROWD

My mother, Jean Dell'Oro, used to always tell a story about an Aramco reunion years ago. At the event's dinner reception, the president of the company was introduced on stage and made a speech. As the crowd applauded, he stepped down, and Ali Baluchi was introduced. The crowd roared for Ali; clearly everyone loved him.

FRED BLANCHARD COMMENTS ON
SHARING COMMONALITY OF ACHIEVEMENT

Over the years since our retirement, we would meet at reunions in America and Saudi Arabia and fondly recall the past and those with whom we shared the commonality of achievement. He would be the first to tell you it wasn't him but the people he led that deserve the credit, a value admired by those who know him.

MOHAMMED AL KHALFAN REFLECTS ON VOLUNTEERING DURING THE 2019 KSA REUNION

During the 2015 Saudi Aramco KSA Reunion, I was surprised to encounter this energetic, big-hearted gentleman, who was then in his late 70s. I ran into him again in Austin, Texas in 2018 at another retiree reunion and was once again impressed by his stamina and meticulous attention to detail as he enthusiastically encouraged his listeners to return to Saudi Arabia for the next annuitant event.

When Ali speaks about Saudi Aramco and his own history with the company, he presents an engaging story, bringing the past vividly to life with his own unique blend of humility and sincere emotion. He certainly knows how to capture the minds and hearts of his audience.

I volunteered to lead trips during the 2019 KSA Reunion and again experienced Ali's attention to detail. While constantly monitoring the 100+ activities taking place, he always checked in with me in particular to particularly ensure the health, safety and comfort of our guests, especially the elderly.

Working alongside Ali, one is also inspired by his wisdom, his passion for the history of Saudi Aramco, and his intense appreciation of life and the people around him.

I discovered that many annuitants and brats consider his friendship to be one of the most cherished aspects of the time they spent in Saudi Arabi.

Respected by Saudis and other nationalities alike, he is truly an extraordinary man and a wonderful friend. We pray that God continues to give him good health and strength.

~ 18 ~

KIND WORDS FROM FAMILY AND FRIENDS

"FATHER" ...

The most beautiful word that my tongue ever spoke;
The most precious feelings that fill my heart:
Your smile makes me happy.
You were, and always will be, my example.
Your kindness and tenderness makes me feel safe
*   and peaceful.*
I appreciate and value all that you have offered me
*   in my life —*
It is the source of my success and my self-confidence.
My prayer to God is to be the person you wished me to be
While blessing you with health and well-being.
You are my father, my friend, my trip companion and
*   my role model.*

YOUR DAUGHTER, AISHA

If the global Aramco family has a father figure, then surely that person is Ali Al-Baluchi. As the driving force, heart and soul of the four expatriate reunions held in Saudi Arabia, no one has done more to bring us all together to celebrate our common experience as Aramcons.

Ali's own career embodies the spirit and can-do attitude of early Aramco. Joining the company in 1949 as an office boy, he rose to become general manager of Community Services, earning two college degrees along the way. People like Ali set a very high standard for succeeding generations of Aramcons, and all of us are indebted to him and our other pioneers for building such a firm foundation for the company's current — and future — success.

Beyond Ali's contributions to the business of Aramco, his generosity of spirit and inclusiveness truly set him apart. Traveling the world after he retired, attending Aramco reunions, he was asked again and again about the possibility of returning to Saudi Arabia. His answer was yes and, summoning that can-do attitude, and with the help of volunteers, local businesspersons and the government, he made it happen — four times!

It's not just the Aramco family that benefits from Ali's big-heartedness. His generous spirit also enlivens cities and towns in the Eastern Province. Ali is like a big bridge that connects multiple generations, cultures and communities with each other, and it's my honor and pleasure to add my voice to the chorus of people who thank Ali for his service and his commitment.

AMIN NASSER, CEO, SAUDI ARAMCO

I'm so thankful and proud for having a grandfather such as mine, he's truly my inspiration and I hope that one day I can reach to what he has achieved. He's the person who, whenever I stumble in life, I find him by my side supporting me. He will always be my motivation to do better and never give up.

YOUR GRANDDAUGHTER, MARIAM HUSSAIN AL-BALUCHI

Ali is a bright and shining light to Aramcons the world over, an inspiration to us all. Whenever there's a major annuitants' reunion on the horizon, knowing that Ali will be there always makes me smile, for seeing him again is a guaranteed delight. His warmth and compassion uplift everyone and everything he touches. He's a treasured friend to thousands of Aramcons everywhere. Ali, in short, is a gift from God to all of us.

Ali is an ambassador for Aramco and the Kingdom. I≈admire Ali and his family for always loving people without being judgmental. He knows what is important to all people, including their religion, country and family.

VICCI TURNER, ARAMCOEXPATS.COM

Being a "people person," Ali's kindness proves he is also very sincere in wanting nationalities of all kinds to unite and be happy. He "bridged the gap" for many expatriates by making them feel so welcome in his country, me for one. He was nice and pleasant to work for, and I know other employees of his felt the same way as me. He was

*certainly a leader in wanting expatriates to know that,
even though our religions were not the same, our hearts
were. His heart was shared by him with a lot of others
and Ali will always be a big part of our memories of
Saudi Arabia.*

PEGGY SMITH, FORMER COLLEAGUE IN
COMMUNITY SERVICES

*Ali has found the perfect vehicle to keep in touch with his
army of friends across the globe — Facebook! Whenever
I visit the site, I see him connecting, always in a positive
way. It could be for a birthday or to offer condolences,
congratulations, encouragement. It seems that any
Aramcon, anywhere, and their kids, are part of his Aramco
family. I think the kids (or "brats") are especially grateful
he is there as gatekeeper, keeping the door open to the
place many still consider as home.*

MARY NORTON, FAMILY FRIEND

*Through the years, you meet a lot of different kinds
of people. Where some change their behavior and
attitudes over time, Ali has not changed at all. This man
is kind, people-loving, generous, human, supportive,
understanding, good-hearted, forgiving [and] tolerant,
and, most of all, treats everyone with respect. Those who
knew his parents know where all this came from.*

*Ali is a veritable school of knowledge, and my
neighborhood friends and I have learned a lot from him.*

He was, and still is, something of an idol to many of us. However, one thing we did not like was when Ali returned from the United States and started wearing short pants. We looked at him with astonishment! I recall his Vauxhall auto, the first car he acquired after coming back from America. He would always take us in his car on Friday afternoons to the club to prepare for a soccer game. Everyone respected Ali.

He has been a great ambassador for Saudi Arabia in relation to building friendly US-Saudi relation. He has done a lot in that area on an individual basis.

DR. IBRAHIM AL-MUTRIF, FORMER ASSOCIATE PROFESSOR AT KING FAHD UNIVERSITY OF PETROLEUM AND MINERALS

I know very little about his work with Aramco, but as a person Ali Baluchi has been a paragon of the virtue of cultivating and maintaining meaningful and sincere friendships. His qualities as a human being are to be cherished, emulated and greatly admired. He is a very special man who richly deserves our great respect and love.

RICHARD HARTZELL, FAMILY FRIEND FROM COLLEGE DAYS

Ali is very keen and has always had an excellent memory, remembering people's names, events and places. I have always envied Ali for his incredible energy. He is people-oriented and goes out of his way to help others as much as he can, and sometimes beyond that, to the extent he gets

*into trouble for it. He is definitely outspoken. Sometimes
I feel he is misunderstood when being aggressive and
blunt, but in reality he means good, although he is
sometimes criticized for being too pushy. He certainly
does not drop the ball, and is always available to pursue
matters to the end. He speaks his mind, even if that gets
him into hot water.*

AHMED AL-HAZZA, LIFELONG FRIEND

*An unwavering and indomitable commitment to the goal
of helping Aramcons come together as a community is
Ali's legacy, and he gets so much pleasure from achieving
that goal. His spirit is contagious, and we all get caught
up in his enthusiasm. Also, his ability to overcome
obstacles put in the way, which he does with humor
and aplomb!*

**JULIE EVELAND, VOLUNTEER PUBLICITY LEAD,
2015 KSA REUNION**

*I was the Saudi Aramco Preventive Dentistry Coordinator
from 1984 to 1997. I'm not sure how our paths crossed;
perhaps Ali was a patient of mine or one of my dental
projects involved his department. Regardless, I still
remember his face and especially his smile. He expressed
sincere interest in what I was doing for the company and
went so far as to suggest that he and I could turn some
of my ideas into a private business to benefit individuals
outside of the Saudi Aramco family. He was always*

thinking of projects to help people and that (as well as his smile and voice) is how I remember him most.

I have no doubt that Ali remembers me and my wife, Rosemary MacIntyre, who managed the Executive Health Program. He has that wonderful gift of remembering people and making them feel important, which is why he is someone you would never forget.

MARTIN MACINTYRE, SAUDI ARAMCO

MEDICAL SERVICES ORGANIZATION

I was first introduced to Ali by mutual friends in the Dhahran Dining Hall when I joined Aramco as a Petroleum Engineer on December 12, 1966. From the first moments of meeting him, I knew he was a person I would always love and trust. He was like a brother to me. I found him honest, pleasant, modest and fair. Being courageous, he seemed to have "no fear" when facing tough situations or people. In his position in Community Services management, he dealt with people at all levels and gained the respect of all, which was no small feat.

DR. RUWAID AHMED AKKAD,

RETIRED COLLEAGUE AND FRIEND

By nature, Ali is a sincere, friendly and gregarious individual. The least that can be said about him is that he loves people and is loved by all in return. It is amazing how he remembers the names of so many people and also the names of their children. Our very dear friend is kind,

generous, sincere and a "go getter." He is a goal-oriented
person both in the work environment and in social relations.
He is a modest and very respectful friend of everyone. I know
of no one who holds ill feelings about Ali. How fortunate!

MOHAMMED SAEED AL-ALI,
LONG-TIME COLLEAGUE AND FRIEND

Ali is generous, perceptive, and always considerate.
I have known him as a hard-working person with
resolve, stamina, professional clarity and dedication,
creativity, fairness and the utmost strongly felt respect
to the individuals who worked with him or have known
him. Some striking characteristics of his personality
include this strongly felt passion towards society and
people of all walks of life, and the driving of creative and
leading initiatives of multicultural significance which
bring together friends despite the challenges of life.
His commitment to the nourishing of ongoing human
relations has a positive and optimistic impact. In that
endeavor, he is conspicuously meticulous.

DR. AHMED AL-SHUWAIKHAT,
MEMBER OF THE SHURA COUNCIL OF SAUDI ARABIA

I was secretary to the Manager of Southern Area
Community Services from about 1987 until 1994. I also
worked in the Abqaiq Housing Office between 1984 and
1987. Ali was the heart of Community Services and was
always just a joy to have visit to our office or our home.

I always look forward to attending reunions because Ali and his lovely wife will be there too.

VIRGINIA READ, FORMER COLLEAGUE AND FAMILY FRIEND

I met Ali in June 2000 and was immediately struck by his command and knowledge of the Amusement Park business and his willingness to listen, ask intelligent questions and come to decisive decisions.

Ali is one of the most gracious people I have had the pleasure to know. I admire his humility and strength, his genuine concern for people, and his fairness and willingness to listen before making a decision. His leadership skills coupled with a resolve to stay current with issues and progress left a lasting impression on me.

DAVID CASCIOLI, LONG-TERM
BUSINESS ASSOCIATE AND FRIEND

There are many things that impress me about Ali. Most of all, his friendliness, social skills and activism in voluntary work. His enduring legacy is his ability to maintain good enduring friendships with so many people and manage to remain in contact with them.

SAUD AL-ASHGAR, FORMER COLLEAGUE
AND FELLOW RETIREE

Ali has a razor-sharp memory; he not only remembers faces but names as well. He is also very wise and intuitive.

We've worked together on several reunions throughout the years and he is tireless — he has a lot of energy and wants things done quickly. He is the blend of being patient and impatient at the same time!

I also love how he genuinely cares about his many friends all over the world. He takes the time to get to know one's life story, no matter how young or old. He has enormous compassion for those who have had hardships and is earnestly happy for those who have good fortune.

I love hearing Ali's stories of when he was a young Aramco employee and how he would hustle to get a job done, even if it meant to only get a few hours of sleep — sometimes driving to Riyadh to pick up an item and driving back to Dhahran before work started. That is the high level of his work ethic and rigor, and if you are working with him, he expects you to do the same.

Ali's legacy is one of an extraordinary man, one who opened not only his heart but also his country to his friends around the world who share his love for the Kingdom. I cherish our friendship and am thankful for who he is and all he has done. Over the years he has been my mentor, leader, friend, hero, confidant and inspiration. I consider him family.

CHERI SANER, ARAMCO "BRAT" AND VOLUNTEER
MARKETING LEAD FOR KSA REUNIONS

Throughout our two decades of friendship, Ali has been an unshakable pillar to his community, expatriate friends

*and even those within friends' extended circles. Ali never
met a stranger. As an employee in the early Aramco days,
he developed a genuine fondness for the expatriates who
passed through his life. He loves to share stories of the
expats with whom he has or had a close relationship.*

*When a memory moves him, Ali narrates vivid scenes
in which he fondly recalls the actions and reactions of
specific individuals, often Americans, who left an indelible
imprint on his life. Having studied in the US, Ali was
indoctrinated as a young man into the spirit of American
ideals and way of life. The friendships he forged were more
than just fond memories of his early career or school days,
they were unbreakable bonds. Ali worked hard during his
tenure in Community Services to build bridges within the
Aramco community, leveraging diversity as strength rather
than viewing it as a challenge.*

*Ali continues his efforts to build on his friendships,
keeping them strong, yet also striving to further expand
his network. To this day, Ali calls his friends, bestowing
upon them warm wishes for the holidays and special
occasions, inquiring about loved ones, and making sure
everyone is in good health. Nearly every year Ali makes
a point to tour the US, stopping to see his friends around
the country, and nurturing the friendships that mean so
much to him. Baba Ali is the patriarch of his large beloved
family, but his extended family includes all whom he holds
dear and those who consider him a friend.*

*I recall shortly after the events of 9/11, Ali had just
returned from one of his stateside visits. I was at work
when he called. As we were talking, I realized Ali was*

very, very sad — perhaps the first time he had let his guard down for me to see. I felt he was close to tears. He proceeded to tell me about his trip. Ali was always meticulous about planning his trips to the US and letting his friends know the dates he would be there. But on this trip, when he called to confirm exact arrival dates and times, he was met with several responses from friends who were either busy or had other excuses why they could not see him. If it had only been one person, or if they were surprise visits, Ali would have been disappointed, but accepted the reality. However, Ali was crushed to be greeted with negative feelings from those he considered friends, all because he represented the Kingdom. Such a situation might have made most individuals reluctant to continue their annual journeys to the US. However, this was not the case with Ali. He soon picked up where he left off and continued to build on both old and new friendships in the US and elsewhere.

As a leader, Ali is the quintessential diplomat, providing quiet guidance and motivating his team to take the lead. For some, he comes across as a very formidable man, but for those who have been fortunate to get to know him well, they see only a genuine man with a huge heart that does not discriminate. No matter the type of concern or problem you might face, Ali has always been there to show his support and let you know that he cares.

KATHLEEN OWEN, FORMER COLLEAGUE, FAMILY FRIEND, AND EVENTS LEAD, KSA REUNIONS

When we moved to Switzerland for seven years, Ali knew where to find us. His loving kindness and delight in learning opened a whole distant world and taught us all about the ties that bind our peoples. He is a gift from God.

NANCY WASHBURNE

In 2008, when I was conducting research for my first novel, I had the pleasure of staying with Ali and his wife Anisa at their home in Al-Khobar. At the time, my father was working for The Zamil Corporation (ZamCo), and they couldn't house visiting family members, so Ali and Anisa opened their home to me. Though I hadn't seen Ali for years and had only vague memories of him from my childhood, he treated me like a daughter, inviting me to share meals with him and his extended family and recounting stories about earlier Aramco days. Ali's wife Anisa didn't speak English, but she was such a kind soul, her warmth emanating from her gestures and care for me during my stay. I will always be grateful to Ali for his generosity to me during that trip back home to Saudi Arabia.

I remember he told me a touching story about how he used his first paycheck to buy his father a watch. He carries within him the human history of the company; the stories he tells are of infinite value to our understanding of the Saudi-American partnership and how it was conducted "on the ground" among employees who came together to do difficult work despite vastly different backgrounds. Ali is a loyal man of deep faith and unwavering conviction in the goodness of the work he was doing. He believed in and loved his country and served it well through his important work for Aramco. But he also believed in and loved the Americans he worked alongside, and he labored tirelessly to ensure that Aramco's American employees felt welcomed, valued and comfortable. I know he handled a lot of sensitive situations, and while I don't know all the details, I'm sure he handled them with grace and dignity and care, doing what was right with great thoughtfulness. Ali is a beloved member of the Aramco community, and I feel grateful that my family came into his orbit during our time in Saudi Arabia.

KEIJA PARSINNEN, ARAMCO "BRAT"

AND FAMILY FRIEND

Ali was a good friend of the family and we remember him as being kind, helpful and sociable, always with a smile on his face. He did a lot for the Ras Tanura community. We wish him the best!

THE GERNONS FAMILY, FRIENDS FROM RAS TANURA DAYS

Ali represents the best of the qualities of open-minded hospitality and intelligent friendship, attributes that are most highly valued throughout the world.

DR. SADAD AL-HUSSEINI, FORMER EXECUTIVE VP OF

SAUDI ARAMCO AND LONG-TERM FRIEND

ODE TO ALI BY ALISON HOOKER

This was written during the 2015 KSA Reunion
to honor Ali Baluchi

If your path has crossed dear Ali's
Then you will surely know
When he wants to make "it" happen,
"It" will surely go!
He has a way of working
That leaves you in no doubt —
His plans will clearly come to pass
And find a gainful route!

But what is it that makes him reach
Across the sands of time
To touch so many hearts and lives
No longer in their prime?
What is the thing that drives him on
To join them overseas,
And gather friends from far and wide
To reunite with ease?

How does he motivate and lead
A team both old and young
Who hail from all the globe around
And toil for praise unsung?
What is this magic sense he has
That all shall come to pass?
A quiet confidence and strength,
A self-belief steadfast.

There are so many qualities
Of his that claim respect:
An active mind, perspective clear,
Ability to connect.
Much energy and wisdom rich,
Loyalty deep and true,
A love of family, national pride,
Company man right through.

But most of all we hold him dear
For his kind and gen'rous heart
That reaches out across the world
To draw friends long apart.
These Gath'rings nurtured by his hand
Are blessed by his great care,
And demonstrate to everyone
A fellowship most rare.

For Ali also understands
That in this changing world
Friendship is a powerful tool,
A flag to keep unfurled.
So when we see our common ground
And think on life we've shared,
We all can raise a prayer of thanks —
Most of all that Ali cared.

POSTSCRIPT

I FEEL IT IS BECOMING increasingly important for those of us with decades of life and work experience to share those lessons we have learned along the way with younger generations. We should also preserve these valuable insights for the future. This was my motivation in writing my memoir. As you have read and reflected on my story, I hope you found some helpful guidance or inspiration to apply into your own life. That will be my legacy to you.

From when I first started traveling for my education, I loved being around people of different backgrounds than my own, taking the opportunities on offer to develop new friendships. Over time, my relational approach even became a career asset, a style and approach I became well known for. I do not judge my friends by their religion, race or gender, and I work hard to keep those most precious relationships fresh and current. I still harbor a wish to visit some of the countries I have not yet traveled to in order to catch up with Saudi Aramco retirees so that we might generate and maintain stronger ties among them.

Another ongoing desire of mine is to meet with more young people as I so enjoy sharing my life experiences with them. I feel they would benefit from considering some of the lessons of my generation. When I was young, I had to work hard at getting my education, and put in a lot of extra effort to improve my skills and gain promotions. I spent my lunch hours going through the Lead Typist Clerk's trash in order to find work to copy so I could practice my typing. I learned to be patient and to work harder than my colleagues so as to gain promotions.

Our society is changing rapidly. In view of this, my wish for my grandchildren and their generation is that they show respect and kindness to their parents and make every effort to educate themselves. They need to become more aware of their communities and where, within their capabilities, they can serve and help others. While I encourage them to take full advantage of the many opportunities they are offered, they should also endeavor to live fruitful lives, giving something back. Likewise, their parents should engage with their children in such a way as to generate a peaceful and constructive environment within the family.

I find great comfort and inspiration from the Quran, but I would like to finish with some passages that are always present in my thoughts:

Chapter 7 Al-Araf, Verse 31: "O children of Adam, take your adornment at every masjid, and eat and drink, but be not excessive. Indeed, He likes not those who commit excess."

Chapter 109 Al-Kaferoun, Verse 6: "For you is your religion, and for me is my religion."

Chapter 4 Al-Nisa', Verse 86: "And when you are greeted with a greeting, greet (in return) with one better than it or (at least) return it (in a like manner). Indeed, God is ever, over all things, an accountant."

ALI MOHAMMED AL-BALUCHI

ACKNOWLEDGMENTS

MY STORY would not have been complete without my dear family members: my parents; my three wives — Sharifa, Anisa (both deceased) and Amira; my sister Fatima and her family; my brothers Abdul Rahman and Jassim and their families; and my children, grandchildren and great-grandchildren.

I would like to acknowledge the endless support I have received over the years from my many friends, from both Saudi Arabia and elsewhere in the world. I thank my American friends who opened their hearts and their homes while I spent many formative and fruitful years among them as a young man. Some became like surrogate parents to me and I still hold them close to my own heart.

I would also like to express appreciation to all of my immediate supervisors at Aramco for their generosity in extending candid suggestions and encouragement to help me mature into the opportunities offered me throughout my career and service to Saudi Aramco.

I must mention those many employees who made me look good in the eyes of management through the decades of my career! Through my own years of dedicated leadership, I appreciated all the excellent work my teams performed and their patience and fortitude in bearing with all the challenges of being trained and developed to improve the delivery of daily tasks and services.

I hope the Saudi Aramco Retirees Advisory Committee will continue its good work. I extend my heartfelt thanks to the hardworking planning committees of the four KSA Reunions: in 2000, 2009, 2015 and 2019. Much appreciation goes to Ahmed Al-Yahyaie for making the soccer tournaments a reality.

I was very touched by all those who took time to share some memories with us for this publication and by the many supportive messages I received for this project.

I am most appreciative of the tireless scholarly work of Dr. Jassim M. Al-Ansari, Dr. Abdullah Al-Madani and Yousif Al-Mulla. Each has made an invaluable contribution to recording the history and development of the Eastern Province, immortalizing it for future generations.

I am most grateful to Robert Lebling and Lorne Christenson for their constructive input; Osama Kadi and the Saudi Aramco Media Production Division for help with sourcing images; Cheri Saner and Art Clark for photographs; and Waleed Dashash for cover photographs. I greatly appreciate time given by Mrs. Basma Fadeel Hamad in helping with translations.

Finally, my particular thanks go to my editor, Mrs. Alison Hooker, who gave endless hours to bring the concept of this book to a reality. Her dedication is appreciated from the bottom of my heart.

May God bless them all!

INDEX

Roman numerals in capitals refer to the introductory pages. Roman numerals in *italics* refer to pages in the plate sections.